MW01624487

Awesome Facts for Disney Fans

The Unofficial Collection

The Encyclopedia of
Secret Knowledge about the
Factory of Dreams

NUCLEO

© 2023 Nucleo
Edition 2.0A

Author:
Lisa Marie Bopp

Verlag:
Nucleo – a label of

my dna media GmbH
Ohmstr. 53
60486 Frankfurt am Main, Germany

ISBN:
978-3-98561-053-2

This book is not an officially licensed product and is not affiliated with The Walt Disney Company or any other Disney rights holder.

This work, including its parts, is protected by copyright. Any usage without the consent of the publisher and the author is prohibited. This applies in particular to electronic or other reproduction, translation, distribution, and public availability.

Unless otherwise noted, year references always apply to the first release date in the United States.

All provided information without guarantee.

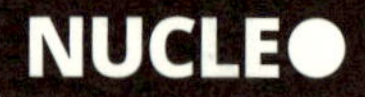

Feedback, Questions, Suggestions?

Get in touch with us at **info@nucleo-media.com** or visit our homepage **nucleo-media.com**

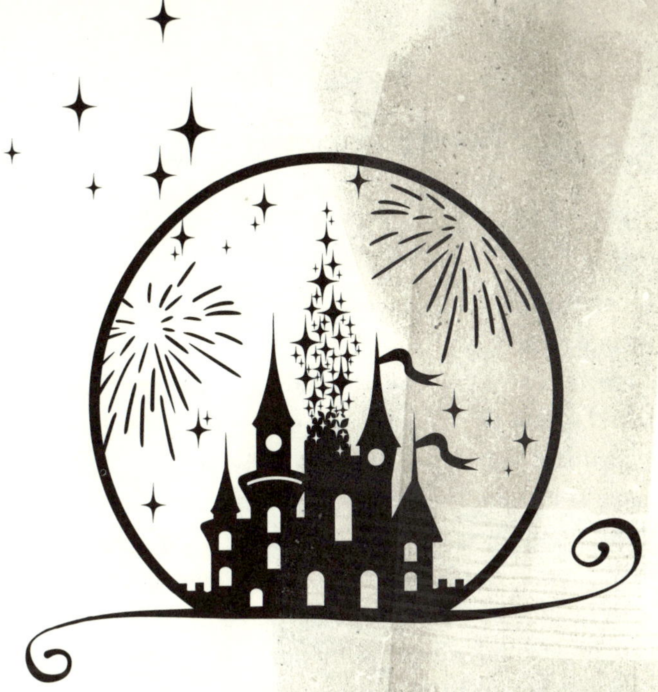

On his 50th birthday, Mickey Mouse received an extraordinary present. The little mouse was awarded a star on the famous Walk of Fame in Hollywood. Mickey was the first animated character on which this honor was bestowed.

From Newspapers to the Big Screen

When Walter Elias Disney was born on December 5, 1901, no one could have imagined that the whole world would know his name one day. Nor did anyone suspect that he would invent the most famous mouse in the world. However, his talent for drawing quickly became apparent. Even as a child, the young Walt was enthusiastic about drawing and had planned to become a cartoonist for a newspaper. Yet, his ultimate breakthrough did not come with newspapers but on the big screen. His first studio, Laugh-o-Gram, which he founded in Kansas, was not very successful. During the early days, the studio even had to rely on the financial support of Walt's brother Roy. The tide turned when Walt decided to try his luck in Hollywood. To finance the trip, he sold his beloved camera and traveled to the West coast of America with only 40 dollars on hand. Luckily, he could live with his uncle at first, which naturally came in handy. This move was the starting point for Disney's worldwide success.

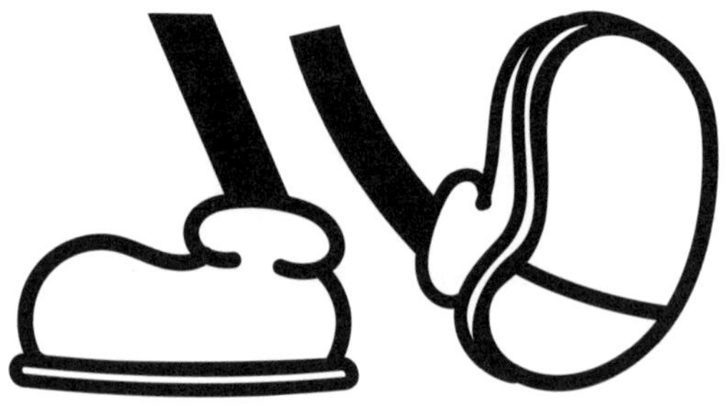

Color Film for Beginners

In Disney's early days, all films were still exclusively in black and white. The first Disney cartoon in color was called *Flowers and Trees*, earning the House of Mouse its first Oscar in the category "Best Animated Short Film." Nowadays, such a film would probably no longer inspire audiences since the plot primarily revolves around dancing trees and flowers, but it was considered highly entertaining at the time.

May the Graphics Be with You

Pixar is known today for classics such as *Finding Nemo, Toy Story,* and *Cars*. The studio's beginnings can be traced back to a subcontractor that was assigned to the graphics department of Lucasfilm – the studio that created the *Star Wars* films. At the time, the department had little to do with animation. It worked much more on special effects and graphic technology jumps. After Lucasfilm started making less money in the mid-1980s, George Lucas planned to sell off the subcontractor. In 1986, Steve Jobs – Apple founder and inventor of the iPhone – bought out the sub-company and renamed it Pixar. Nowadays, the studio is part of the Walt Disney Company.

Success After 70 Years

Walt Disney had the first ideas for the movie *Frozen* back in the 1930s. Strictly speaking, work on the animated hit lasted more than 70 years. During that time, the project was repeatedly dropped and taken up again until the moment finally came in 2013, when the film came onto the big screen – a complete success! Although Walt Disney could no longer witness this triumph, without his preliminary work and the original idea, it might have never come to the film's release.

The Lost Nephew

If you're convinced that taking care of three kids isn't always an easy job, you're sure to find Donald Duck to agree. But if three children can be exhausting – then what about four? Donald Duck can certainly also have an opinion on this matter. After all, strictly speaking, he has four nephews, doesn't he? Huey, Dewey, and Louie should be well-known to most fans. But here and there, a fourth nephew appears: Phooey. The fourth among the brothers should probably not exist at all but was drawn in by a comic artist (probably by mistake) in one of the stories in 1999. Since then, Phooey has appeared from time to time, or allusions have been made to him, yet he remains a minor mystery in the Duckburg world.

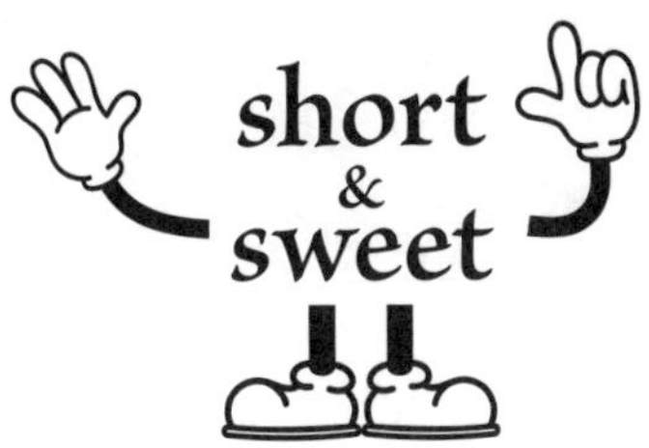

Already at the age of 16, Walt Disney wanted to enlist for military service. But since he was still too young, he was refused entry. However, he found an alternative: He became an ambulance driver during the First World War.

Comedian and actor Steve Martin worked as a Disneyland employee before his big break. He had a position in the Magic Shop.

Originally, the teapot from *Beauty and the Beast* was supposed to be called Mrs. Chamomile. But since that was difficult for many to pronounce, it was changed to Mrs. Potts.

Buzz Lightyear in a red spacesuit? It almost came to that because the *Toy Story* hero's color palette was only later changed to the purple and green that we know today.

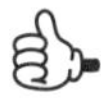

Mickey Mouse was created in 1928 by Ub Iwerks and Walt Disney.

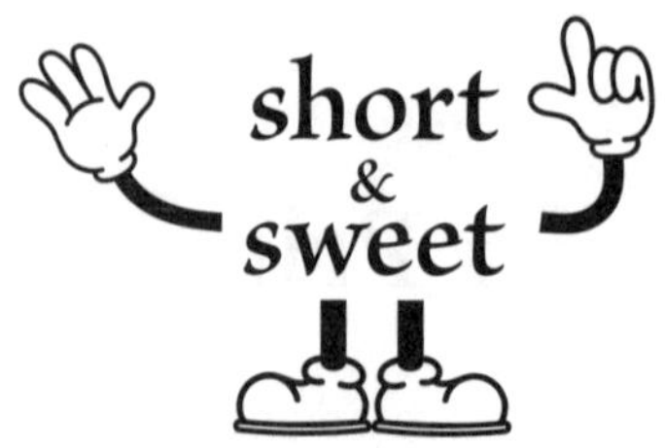

You don't have to pay for drinking water at Disney World. Every drink stand gives out free water if you ask for it.

In 1937, Walt Disney released its first fully animated film *Snow White* with a running time of 83 minutes.

The founders of Disney were the brothers Walt and Roy Disney. While Walt was mainly responsible for the animations, his brother Roy took care of the business end of the company.

Although Disneyland was supposed to be only open for the press on its opening day on July 17, 1955, many other people were at the park that day. The uninvited guests even jumped over the fence or got counterfeit tickets to see the park.

Disney founder Walt Disney died of lung cancer in 1966.

Criteria for Princesses

The Disney princesses are among the best-known and most popular characters in the Disney films. However, to be accepted into this exclusive club and actually be allowed to officially call yourself a Disney princess, there are certain requirements to be met. The criteria are clearly defined by Disney. It is important that the aspirant be either of royal birth or becomes a princess by marrying a prince. However, there is one exception: Although Mulan is not a princess of royal birth, she officially belongs to the group. Disney justifies this by saying that Mulan's glorious actions as well as the fact that she saves her country have honorably elevated her to a princess status. In the case of movies with a sequel, it is crucial for the recognition as a princess that the aspirant is not only introduced in a second part but already plays an important role in the first film. It does not necessarily have to be the leading role, as is the case with Jasmine from *Aladdin*. Furthermore, an official Disney princess should be human or at least human-like. By this rule, Ariel officially qualifies for the group, while Nala from *The Lion King* does not.

Fun fact: Only 13 princesses are officially recognized as Disney princesses. The group includes Snow White, Cinderella, Aurora, Ariel, Belle, Jasmine, Mulan, Pocahontas, Rapunzel, Tiana, Merida, Moana, and Raya.

What Is the Name?

Finding a name for a large company is apparently not that easy. And being happy with that name even after a few years, even less so. Bearing that in mind, it's unsurprising that media giant Disney has changed its name several times. Initially, the company was called Disney Brothers Cartoon Studio until it was renamed The Walt Disney Studio in 1926. Only three years later, the next name change occurred, this time to Walt Disney Productions. Since 1986, the company has been called The Walt Disney Company. Let's see if it stays that way...

The First Words

Disney was already producing successful films when they were still mostly black and white and silent. Gradually, film technology developed further, and color and sound films were also established. This meant that Mickey Mouse could finally be given a voice. The previously silent mouse had already been shown laughing, whistling, or crying, but until 1929 he had never spoken. This was to change with the short film *The Karnival Kid* when Mickey spoke for the first time on the screen. His first words were "Hot dog!"

Other Countries, Other Customs...

The creators behind the Disney movies often think up all kinds of things to make a film look realistic. But that doesn't just apply to the animation technology. In some cases, even different details were incorporated into the movie for other countries. In *Inside Out*, for example, there is a scene where Riley refuses to eat her vegetables. While in the version for most countries, she is disgusted by broccoli, she dreads green peppers in the adaptation for Japan. The sports scene in Riley's father's head also changes depending on the country's version. In the US, the father's emotions are diverted to a hockey game; in the UK, a soccer game is to be seen. In total, 28 graphic changes were made in 45 film frames.

The Most Famous Lamp

At the beginning of every Pixar film, a short intro appears with the Pixar lettering and a small lamp bouncing around on the "I." In fact, this lamp is a main character from the studio's short film *Luxo Jr.* It was actually the first short film made under the studio's name and the first to win an Oscar in 1986. The strip, about two minutes long, is about two lamps, one of which – Luxo Jr. – would later become known as Pixar's mascot.

The Car Salesman of Olympus

Fast-talking, wild gestures, and seemingly constantly under stress – that's how viewers got to know the character Hades in the Disney film *Hercules*. However, when the film was still in the planning stages, Hades was attributed to a completely different personality. It was only a certain candidate at the audition for the role that brought about the change: James Woods. He interpreted the character in a completely different way than intended and appeared as a kind of fast-talking car salesman, always with a good line on his lips. Those responsible were so impressed by this casting that they promptly rewrote the character and adapted it to this performance. Otherwise, some of the funny scenes wouldn't have ended up in the film!

Memory Training

If a single specific line from a Pixar movie has been memorized, it's probably "P. Sherman, 42 Wallaby Way, Sydney." The address Dory tries to remember in *Finding Nemo* most viewers know by heart after watching the film. Dory herself names it eleven times in the movie, but she only manages to pronounce it correctly three times.

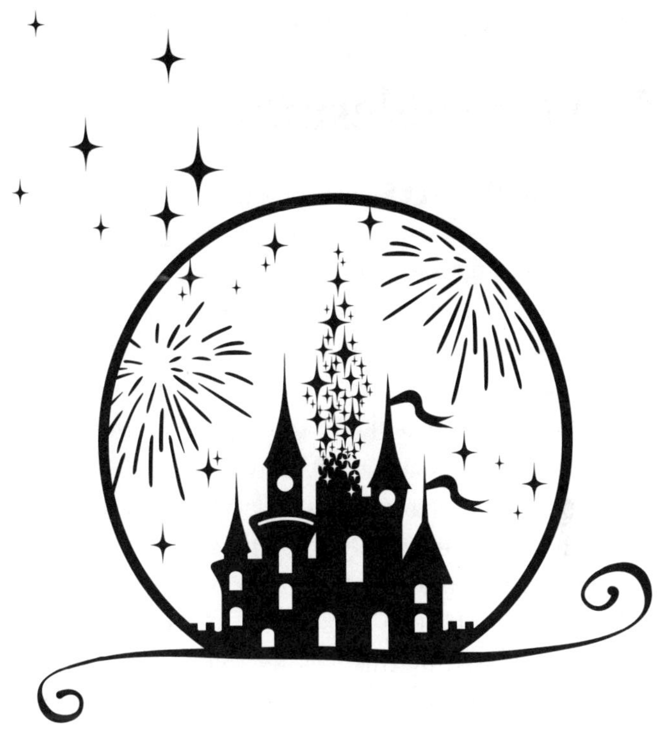

The National Disney Day is celebrated on December 5 – Walt Disney’s birthday.

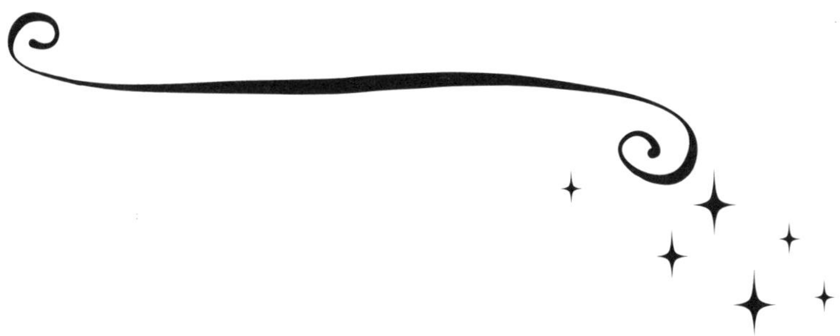

Always on Site

The opening of Mickey Mouse Park in California in 1955 was a great dream come true for Walt Disney. He had once visited Griffith Park in Los Angeles and from then on he had been determined to open his own theme park. Since he was so happy about it and because he wanted to spend most of his time there, he promptly had an apartment built within the park. He and his family could then live in an apartment above the fire department on Main Street. Visitors were also visibly pleased about the park – perhaps because admission was only 2.50 dollars at the time. The park still exists today but now, however, under the name Disneyland. Although Walt Disney's apartment is no longer inhabited, the employees came up with a way to celebrate the late Disney founder: During his lifetime, a light was always burning in a window so that the park workers knew when Walt Disney was on-site. Nowadays, the light burns continuously – in remembrance of him.

Cuddly and Soft

Stubby, blue, and with purple dots – this is the fur of *Monsters, Inc.* star Sully. It makes you want to snuggle right up to him, as soft as it looks! The makers had to animate about 2.3 million individual hairs on his body to convince viewers that the fur is cuddly and looks natural.

Mortimer Mouse

Who doesn't know him – Mortimer? Usually in a good mood and with a laugh that is simply recognized everywhere, he is the mascot of the media giant Disney after all. Wait a minute. Isn't that Mickey Mouse? That's right! Mickey was supposed to be called Mortimer back in the day. But Walt Disney's wife, Lillian Disney, thought the name wouldn't fit well. Thanks to her, the name was changed to Mickey.

From the Park to the Cinemas

Disney is not only famous for its cartoons and animated films. Productions such as the *Pirates of the Caribbean* series also enjoy numerous fans. These franchises are naturally also represented in the Disney Parks. In the case of *Pirates of the Caribbean*, there are two exciting details about the associated park ride. It was the last attraction that founder Walt Disney still personally supervised. If you're wondering how that's possible, since the *Pirates of the Caribbean* films were created after the founder's death (1966), you should read the second interesting detail: It was the park attraction that inspired the filmmakers to bring the adventure to the screen – not the other way around!

Same But Different

Even a large company like the Walt Disney Company must occasionally cut costs. A straightforward way to achieve this is to reuse material. However, this does not mean that films, which have already been released, will be shown in theaters once again. Instead, animations that had already been developed were not only used in one film but in several. It is therefore no wonder that fans are regularly overcome with the feeling that they are already familiar with a scene. Parallels can be found between *Robin Hood* and *The Jungle Book*, as well as between *The Sword in the Stone* and *The Princess and the Frog*. If you look closely, you can spot short sequences in most of the traditionally animated Disney films that appear similarly in other films.

On the Radar

The name Pixar was created when the studio was still part of Lucasfilm. At the time, the team was working on a new computer technology. One employee suggested giving it a cool name and calling it Pixer. The team decided to refine the name and settled on Pixar: *Pix* is a Spanish made-up word meaning pixel and the suffix *-ar* is derived from radar, so Pixel-Radar or Pixar for short.

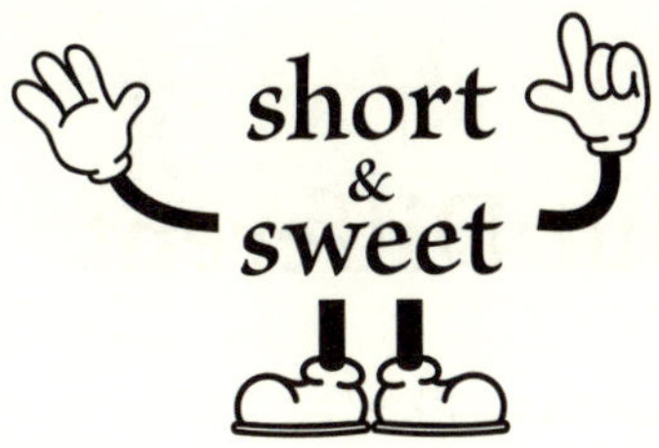

Cinderella wears a size five shoe. No wonder hardly anyone fits into it except for her.

The Incredibles 2 is the longest of the animated Pixar films, with a running time of 118 minutes.

Almost macabre: Disney Parks are considered popular places to scatter the ashes of the deceased.

Real women served as references for the three fairies in *Sleeping Beauty*. The filmmakers oriented themselves primarily toward older, grandma-like women in supermarkets or other public places.

The voice actress who voices Tiana in *The Princess and the Frog* only wanted to accept the role on one condition: Tiana should be left-handed like herself.

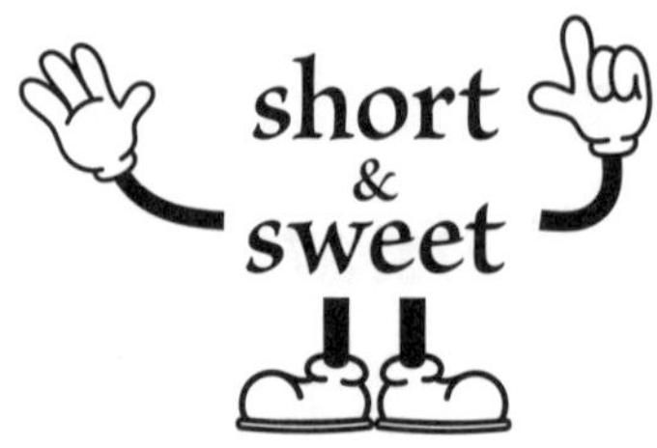

Even though her name is never mentioned, the little girl's real name in *Monsters, Inc.* is revealed. On one of her drawings in her room, she signed Mary.

In *Pocahontas*, a Disney princess has the choice between two men for the first time. If you count the sequel to the film, there are even three men. Despite all this, the chief's daughter decides – at least at the end of the first part – to stay alone.

In 2009, Disney bought out Marvel Entertainment for around four billion dollars. To get hold of the rights to the film adaptations of the Marvel comics, Disney paid not only with hard money but also with a part of its shares.

With *Tangled,* Disney released its 50th animated film. This also makes it the first animated film by the House of Mouse to bring a well-known fairy tale to the big screen by using an entirely new 3D computer technology.

An Intentional Faux Pas

In general, Disney films stand for child-friendly content. At least, this is still true for the cartoons and animated films of the media giant. But even Disney films are allowed a few little jokes here and there, as long as they aren't too bad. In *The Lion King*, for example, it was the first time that a character was allowed to fart in public. Yet, Pumbaa would only be half as funny if this characteristic wasn't integral to his role.

The Most Famous Elephant in the World

It wouldn't have taken much for the cover of the Time magazine to be adorned with an elephant. Once a year, the "Person of the Year" is usually featured here. In 1941, however, an elephant named Dumbo was chosen for this honor. As "Mammal of the Year," the little elephant from the movie of the same name was to be the cover model. The decision had been practically made when at the end of the year an unforeseen tragedy – the attack on Pearl Harbor –caused Dumbo to give up his place. However, he was still honored in the cinema section of the magazine's interior.

The Disney Community

Nowadays, the Epcot area of Disney World in Florida is an area of the theme park with roller coasters, restaurants, and other features. Originally, however, it was planned quite differently. Epcot is an abbreviation for "Experimental Prototype Community of Tomorrow." Initially, a self-contained community was to be built on the site, operating entirely independently, and comprising about 20,000 residents. Shopping facilities, theaters, restaurants, a specially controlled climate, as well as strict planning and control were to be provided to show what life in America's future could be like. However, after the death of Walt Disney, who had pushed the idea, the venture was abandoned because it seemed too unrealistic to those in charge. Instead, Epcot became what it is today: a theme park.

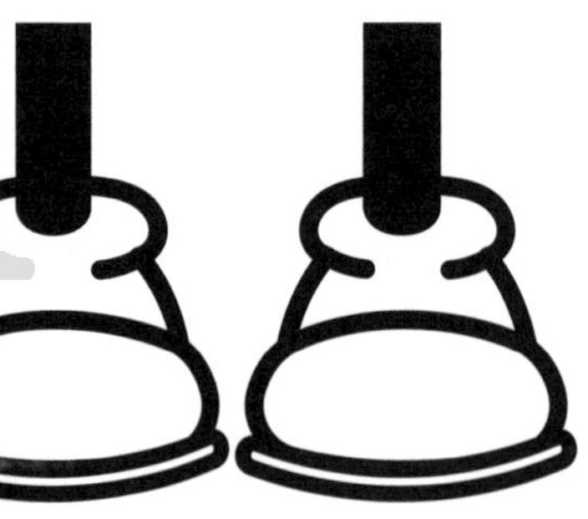

The Creator's Voice

Over the years, Disney's mascot Mickey Mouse has been given several voices. Although the little mouse was still animated silent in its early days, it soon became clear that with the appearance of the talkies, it would also have to be given a voice. At first, it was none other than the Disney founder and Mickey creator himself who took on the voice-over role: Walt Disney. For almost 20 years, he became the voice of the mouse. However, this put immense strain on his vocal cords. The fact that Disney was a heavy smoker was also not conducive to this task. Finally, it made his voice slowly sound rougher and led to frequent coughing, which complicated sound recordings. In 1947, he finally gave up the role.

Technology Makes It Happen

New films also always require new technologies. For *Mulan*, for example, a unique program was developed to represent the armies and crowds in the movie. The program, named Attila – probably in reference to Attila the Hun – allowed the animators to transfer the movements of a single character to large crowds.

Flabby Babies

The story of the movie *Wall-E* takes place several centuries in the future. In the film, humans have left Earth and live in outer space instead. Initially, the filmmakers considered depicting the humans in the movie in an entirely different way. Originally, the humans were supposed to have evolved into boneless blobs in the process. The idea of depicting them as helpless giant babies came later.

The Disney Bunny

It's not for nothing that Disney is also known as the House of Mouse. Of course, the company's mascot Mickey Mouse is responsible for that, although things looked quite different in the early days. Before Mickey entered the world, Oswald the Lucky Rabbit was considered the best candidate for the job. After all, Oswald was the first famous cartoon character created by Walt Disney. However, Walt Disney did not hold the rights to the character, but Universal Studios did. After a dispute, Disney abandoned work on Oswald the Lucky Rabbit. Instead, he wanted to create a character whose rights were his alone. This was the birth of Mickey Mouse.

Disney Style Comic

The good-natured, wobbly robot from the movie *Big Hero 6* is not only a real Disney hero but also a Marvel hero. He originally derived from a Marvel comic called *Big Hero 6*. Of course, Disney won't be expecting any licensing problems since the House of Mouse bought up the comic giant Marvel in 2009. Nevertheless, *Big Hero 6* remains a Marvel story that has been given a film adaptation but was not actually created by Marvel Studios. Regardless, some other Marvel characteristics were retained. For example, comic book legend and superhero creator Stan Lee makes a small cameo appearance, as he does in most other Marvel productions. He is the voice of Fred's father. *Big Hero 6* was also given an additional post-credit scene, which is also typical for Marvel movies.

Special Gift

In the movie *Lady and the Tramp,* a scene shows how Lady comes to the family as a Christmas gift. The scene is actually a tribute by Walt Disney to his wife Lilly and was inspired by a true event. At that time, Walt Disney had given his wife a puppy, hidden in a hat box that he had put under the tree for Christmas. His wife naturally thought there would be a hat inside and was disappointed not to be able to choose the hat herself. When she opened the box, the surprise was all the greater.

Convincing Relationship

The little rabbit Thumper is Bambi's best friend in the film. Originally, he was only planned as a supporting character, receiving far less time in front of the camera. The fact that he appeared in several scenes was due to Walt Disney himself. The Disney founder decided after viewing a common scene of the two that the friendship between deer and rabbit should be a little more present in the film.

Subsequent Change

It is not very often that a character's script is changed in a film that is actually finished. Especially when the animations are already completed, it will take a lot of work to adapt the mouth movements to the new script. A somewhat faster solution is to change the text only slightly and at least keep the length of the respective sentence. This is how it was done in one of *Beauty and the Beast's* final scenes – the fight scene at the castle. Here, Gaston's actual words to the Beast were, "Time to die!" However, it was decided that this statement was too harsh for an animated film. The line was changed to "Belle is mine!" But if you pay close attention, you can see that Gaston's mouth movements still belong to the old line.

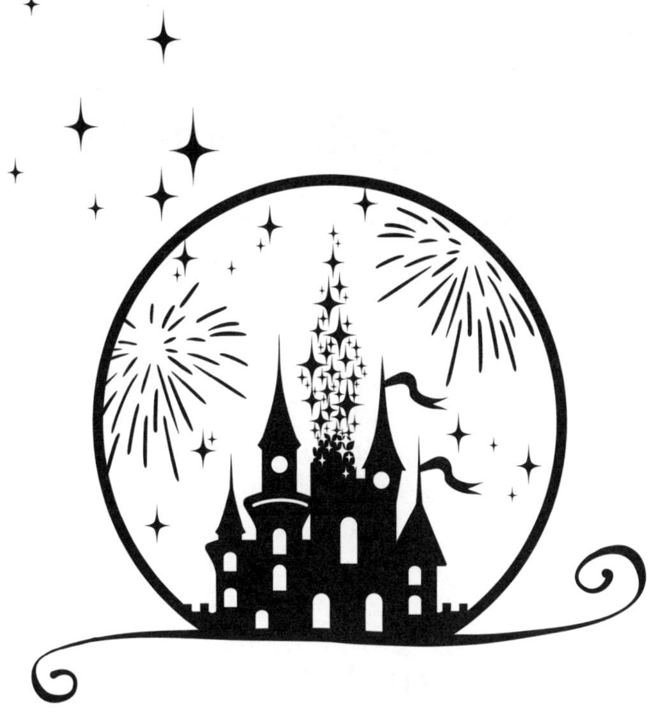

Woodie, the cowboy from *Toy Story,* wasn't even portrayed as a cowboy in the first script. Instead, he took the form of a ventriloquist's dummy. His name was also different at first: He was called Slim.

Of Dogs and Planets

Mickey Mouse has a pet. His dog Pluto has accompanied the little mouse on some of his adventures for many years. If the name of the dog reminds you of the dwarf planet of the same name in our solar system, you are on the right track. Mickey's companion was actually named after the celestial body Pluto. The cartoon dog was created and given its name in 1930 – the same year when the dwarf planet was first discovered.

Infinite Disney

To experience a Disney adventure up close at least once has certainly been a wish of many fans. For a while, this wish was actually quite easy to realize. All you needed was a game console and a game from the *Disney Infinity* video game series. There, players could experience different plots with Disney characters like *The Incredibles*, the monsters from *Monsters, Inc.*, or even the *Pirates of the Caribbean*. Creating your own environment and exploring the Disney world freely was also possible in a separate mode. However, the games are no longer available for purchase, and the online service has also been discontinued. The reason: Disney completely withdrew from the development of video games and dissolved both the development studio and the company for publishing the games.

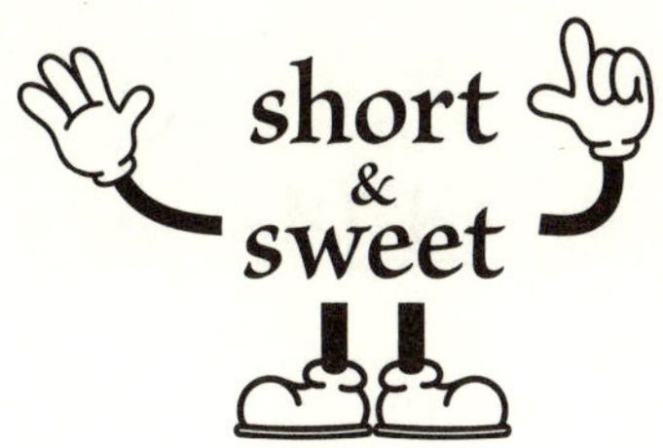

Alice from *Alice in Wonderland* and Wendy from *Peter Pan* share the same voice. The voice is that of Kathryn Beaumont, whom the filmmakers were so impressed with during her work as Alice that they invited her back to the studio two years later for Wendy.

The Disney classic *Bambi* is based on a book. For this reason, it was clear from the beginning that Bambi's mother would die in the film. Even when his daughter asked Walt Disney not to let Bambi's mother die in the movie, the Disney founder was not dissuaded from this plan.

For *The Little Mermaid*, over a million bubbles had to be drawn by hand. This work was hardly manageable for the Disney Studio's animators alone, so the production was partly outsourced to external studios in China.

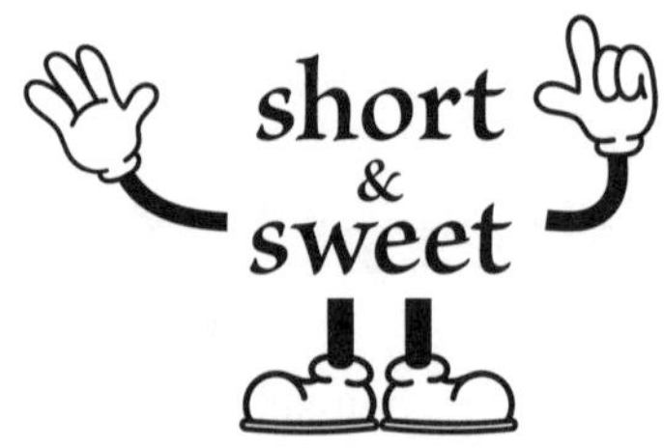

Tim Burton is now a star behind the camera in the film industry. But it all started for the writer, director, and producer at Disney, where he was initially involved as an artist in *The Fox and the Hound*, among other projects.

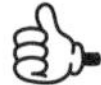

The main music track in the movie *Descendants 2* is inspired by the musical *Hamilton*. Apparently, a good idea since it ranked high in the US music charts.

Since Disneyland California was built on the site of a former orange plantation, the park is mainly dedicated to planting the grounds. The area around The Jungle Cruise ride alone was planted with over 700 species of plants – a beautiful way to make amends.

The fact that the music-loving alligator from *The Princess and the Frog* is named Louis is no coincidence. The name is a tribute to jazz legend Louis Armstrong.

Little Helpers

Two little mice commit themselves to helping others while defying all odds to do so. With this principle, the film *The Rescuers* has been able to convince audiences since 1977. The film was so successful that it received a sequel in 1990 with *The Rescuers Down Under.* This was a first for Disney: The little main characters were the first to be part of a second cinema adaptation. Before then, it was not common for animated films to receive multiple parts. The sequel to the audience's favorite was even more successful than the first part!

The Wrong Hit

Fans of the animated film *Encanto* most likely enjoyed not only the story and its visuals but also the film's songs. The song *We Don't Talk About Bruno* was particularly popular and broke all expectations. For the makers, however, this was not only a reason to celebrate but also quite a disappointment. Since the film was only released at the end of November 2021, they could no longer nominate the popular song for a possible Oscar. The application deadline for this had already expired on November 1. The title that the people in charge had pinned their hopes on and had therefore nominated in advance for the award was *Dos Oruguitas,* which in the end, however, did not win an Oscar for the House of Mouse.

Diversity

With Tiana from *The Princess and the Frog*, Disney introduced its first princess with dark skin. But other ethnicities have also been included among the Disney princesses. For example, Mulan, Jasmine, and Moana represent Asian, Arab, and Polynesian cultures. So, anyone who claims that all princesses must keep to a particular stereotype is proven wrong here.

Hate or Love?

Friendship plays a significant role in many Disney films. Probably the closest friendships of Disney princesses are those between Pocahontas and Nakoma and between Tiana and Charlotte. However, the latter friendship almost didn't happen. Charlotte was originally planned quite differently. Her character was supposed to be a stuck-up, spoiled brat, and Tiana was meant to work for her. The friendship between the two wouldn't have developed at all because they couldn't stand each other in this first draft. Later, however, it was decided to go with the version we know today, and one of the closest Disney friendships was born.

An Important Step

The Oscar is one of the most coveted film awards. However, the trophy – especially in the "Best Film" category – was long considered unattainable for children's films. That only changed with the release of *Mary Poppins*. The film earned the Disney company its first Oscar nomination in this category. Although the film did not ultimately win the award, it was honored in five other categories – including best actress, editing, and song – and was nominated for a total of 13 awards.

Special Hair

An animated film often has to deal with very different challenges compared to a film with real actors. Probably the biggest problem is making the animated characters look as realistic as possible. New techniques are constantly being developed to achieve this. The hair of the Disney princesses is a particularly big challenge. For Merida's wild curls, a special animation technique was developed. After all, it's not that easy to achieve a realistic look for over 1,500 individual strands. In fact, the software used is so successful that Pixar ensured that no other studio could use this technique.

A Voice for Eternity

In animated films, the characters are created exclusively on paper or computer. The voice is recorded later by dubbing actors. This was also the case with *Snow White* in 1937. However, the dubbing artist Adriana Caselotti benefitted far less from it than today's voice actors. Back then, she received a one-time payment of 970 dollars. By now, that would be worth about 17,251 dollars in today's money, but one important little detail was not included in the film: her name in the credits. Due to this small detail she had a hard time getting future jobs in the industry since she couldn't call on her experience with the Disney film. Nowadays, of course, voice-over roles are always included in the credits, and often even prominent voice actors are cast for the characters.

Back Home

Disneyland is divided into different areas, each with a different theme. The Main Street area must have been particularly important to founder Walt Disney. It is modeled after his hometown of Marceline, Missouri, from 1910.

Fun fact: The film *Lady and the Tramp* is also based on this scenario.

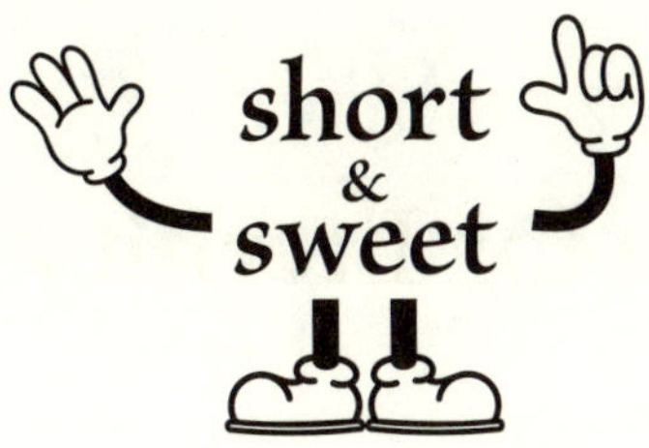

The idea for the Pixar animated film *Up* was inspired by several different movies. The creators wanted to make a film that revolved primarily around character development and took their cues from films like *Casablanca* and *Station Agent.*

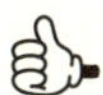

In 1983, Disneyland Tokyo was the first Disney theme park to open its doors outside the United States.

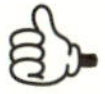

For almost 20 years, *The Lion King* was considered the most successful film for home cinema, with over 55 million copies sold. It wasn't until 2013 that the king was pushed from his throne and replaced by a queen – Elsa from *Frozen* took his place.

Throughout Walt Disney's lifetime, the scatterbrained Goofy was one of his favorite characters.

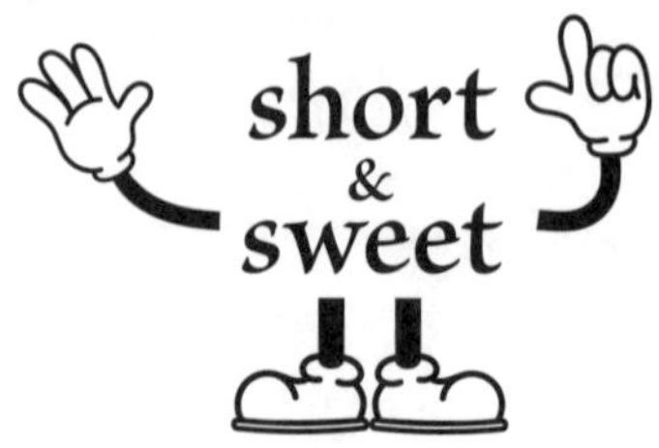

Walt Disney dropped out of school at the age of 16.

Although Elvis Presley made his own movies, none of them contain as many of his songs as *Lilo & Stitch*.

Among other things, Disney films are known for having a certain musical character. For *Tarzan*, however, those responsible wanted to distance themselves from this style and therefore asked Phil Collins to write the music for the film.

The movie *Wall-E* takes place in the year 2805. Nevertheless, during the story, Wall-E finds a game console – an Atari 2600 – which would have to be well over 800 years old at this point.

With an age of only 23, Hans from *Frozen* is the youngest of the Disney villains.

Logo Change

The Disney logo has changed repeatedly over the course of time. Initially, it consisted of the image of a famous character: Mickey Mouse. The company's mascot then had to give way to various other ideas until those responsible finally agreed on the now-familiar Disney castle, complete with star and lettering. This logo has appeared in Disney films since 1985. So the first film to use this identifying feature was *The Black Cauldron*.

Character Search

In every Pixar film, the viewer can embark on a search. Sometimes conspicuous, sometimes well hidden, an Easter Egg can be found in almost every animated film. You should keep your eyes open for the term "A113." There's a little story behind it, of course. A113 is the number of a room at the California Institute of Arts, where many of the Disney and Pixar animators learned and worked. For this reason, the code can also be found in the Pixar films. Sometimes on a wall, sometimes as a license plate or in various other forms. You will find the code if you pay attention to every little detail in the movies.

Made for the Big Screen

When it comes to film sequels, those responsible have to ask themselves a few questions. First of all, it has to be decided whether it's financially worthwhile to release another part of the story. In this context, the decision must be made whether the film should be released in theaters or only as a direct-to-video title – that is, directly for the home screen without a theatrical release. Theatrical movies are usually far more elaborate and, therefore, more expensive to produce, while films made for direct DVD sales are usually not as costly. Moreover, a good profit can be made with direct video sales almost immediately. This very possibility was considered in the early days of *Toy Story 2*. The trigger was the financial success of the direct video production of the *Aladdin* sequel, *The Return of Jafar*. Therefore, the *Toy Story* sequel was originally intended to be released directly on DVD instead of in theaters. In the end, however, the makers decided to produce it as a theatrical film. At any rate, that didn't harm the film's popularity.

Not Made to Measure

Not all attractions found in the Disney Parks were constructed especially for them. For instance, probably the oldest ride in Disneyland, the King Arthur Carousel, was originally made for Sunnyside Beach Park in Toronto.

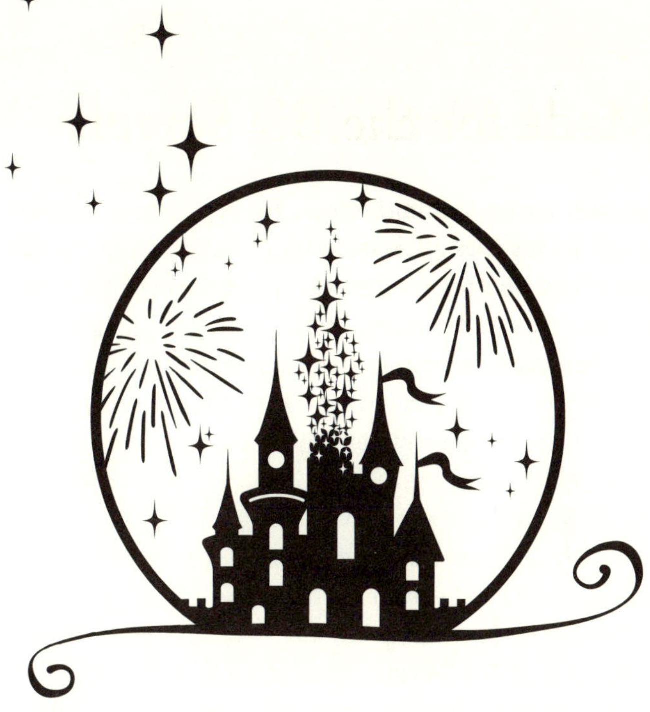

The production costs of *Snow White and the Seven Dwarfs* were way too high for Disney. Therefore, founder Walt Disney had to take a mortgage on his family home to get the project financed.

Smile, Please!

What do you think is the most photographed place in the United States? The Statue of Liberty, perhaps? The Grand Canyon? It's probably impossible to say for sure. What is certain, however, is that Disney World is at the top of the list of potential candidates. Disney's official photographers alone take up to 200,000 photos of guests a day. And that doesn't even include private pictures or social media posts.

For Invited Guests Only

Usually, Disney Parks are mainly a place for children to go. But adults also get their money's worth. Especially if you are a member of Club 33, you have access to a whole lot of amenities. However, only about 500 people can currently enjoy this exclusive service. Membership in the club is strictly limited. It is primarily the stars of the film industry who make their way there. Anyone who wants to have an opportunity of becoming a member has to wait at least 14 years for a place due to the long waiting list.

Awards Earned

Walt Disney never went to university or college. Yet, he has three academic degrees. How is that possible? Through his work. Due to his extraordinary achievements, several universities noticed him and his skills, and as a result three of them awarded honorary degrees to the Disney founder. Walt Disney received a Master of Science degree from the University of Southern California and a Master of Arts degree from the elite universities of Harvard and Yale.

Hidden Mice

If you want to relax a bit at Disneyland and don't feel like sitting non-stop on roller coasters and show grandstands, you can pass the time with something completely different. How about a mouse hunt, for example? The silhouette of the Disney mascot Mickey Mouse is scattered throughout the park and can be found in the decorations, as a detail on the buildings, or even in the shape of some tables. How many hidden mice can be found in total?

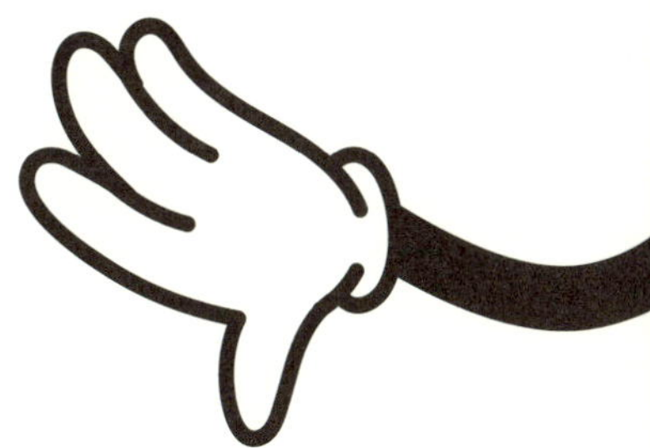

The Pixar Theory

Film fans are always coming up with wild theories. This doesn't just happen with individual films but even with an entire film production house. Disney Pixar is responsible for many animation hits, such as *Finding Nemo*, *Toy Story*, or *Inside Out*. Fans even go as far as to claim that all Pixar films belong together and are set in the same universe, even though some films are set in different places or at different times. According to the Pixar theory, the prehistoric adventure *The Good Dinosaur* forms the beginning, *Brave* is set in the 10th century, *Wall-E* in 2805, and *Monsters, Inc.* even further on in the future, where animals have mutated and formed a society hidden from humans as intelligent monsters. Sounds crazy? Fans of this theory, however, are gathering plenty of evidence and proof. On the website *pixartheory.com*, the fan chronology can be viewed.

Early Practice

Of all the official Disney princesses, Snow White is the youngest at only 14. Just a little older is Jasmine with 15 years. The most senior princess is Tiana aged 19, if you don't count Elsa (21), since she is technically a queen, not a princess, and is not part of the official Disney princess squad.

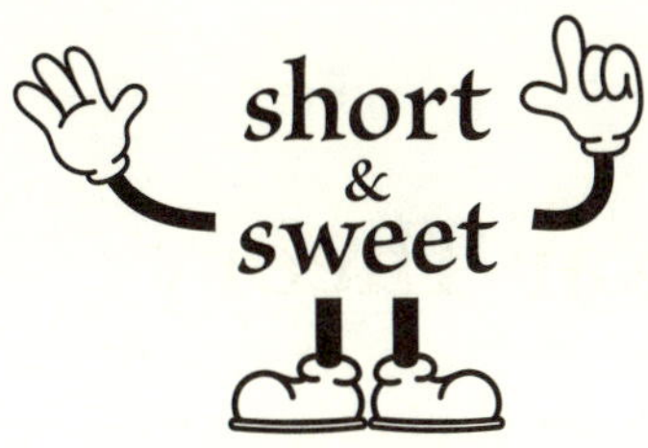

For the movie *Inside Out*, it was originally considered that Riley's childhood friend Bing Bong should be the villain. According to the initial idea, his goal was to keep Riley from growing up.

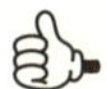

No other Pixar film used as many locations for the story as *The Incredibles*.

The spaghetti scene in *Lady and the Tramp* almost didn't make it into the final film. Walt Disney had it deleted at first but then decided to change his mind after an employee created a rough version of the scene that Walt Disney liked after all.

Fitting to their destination, Lightning and Mater watch a Japanese game show on their way to Tokyo in *Cars 2*. It might also look familiar to older viewers: It's a cars-tuned version of *Takeshi's Castle*.

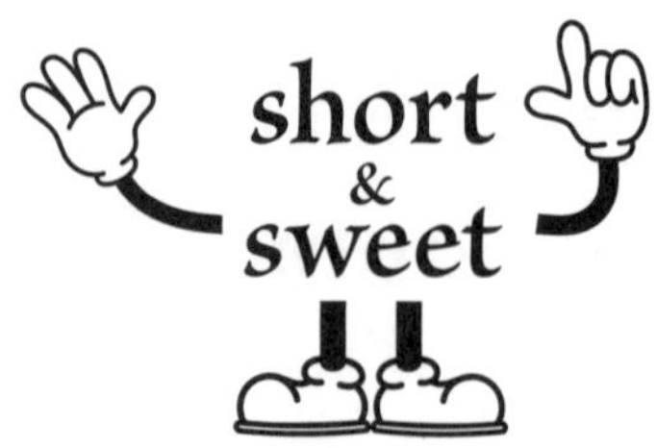

The voice actor who voiced Bambi in the film of the same name, later took on a profession that one would not necessarily associate with the little deer. He became an instructor and made his career in the United States Marine Corps, where he concealed his Bambi past.

Cinderella manages to lose her shoe a whole three times during her film.

Woody from *Toy Story* has a last name: Pride. This secret was revealed on the release of the third *Toy Story* movie. Internally at Pixar, Woody has actually had the last name already since the first part.

A film trailer showing the complete first scene is extremely unusual. But that's exactly what was done for the first trailer for *The Lion King*. Not only were the first images shown, but the scene was also complemented by the accompanying soundtrack, *Circle of Life*.

The Behavior of a Princess

Sometimes, real issues or psychological behaviors are named after famous movie characters. Even Disney princesses are not safe from such references. Cinderella, for example, is the namesake for two psychological conditions at once. On the one hand, the Cinderella syndrome describes a woman who feels emotionally and financially dependent on a man; on the other hand, the syndrome also represents the constant search for the perfect partner, a Mister Perfect or Prince Charming.

Legends among Themselves

The story around Moana and Maui is inspired by the legends and lifestyles of Polynesian cultures. Therefore, the film contains numerous allusions. One example is the animals that Maui can transform into with the help of his hook. For example, a lizard, a whale, or a shark appear more than once. The animals, in turn, have some similarities to mythical creatures in Hawaiian and New Zealand legends. Especially the creatures named Taniwha and Mo'o/Moho were considered by the creators. In the legends, the creatures often have the gift of being able to shape-shift and are considered both destructive forces and protectors of people.

Subsequent Adjustments

Disney came into a bad light in 2013 when the company made some graphic changes to already-known Disney princesses. Both Mulan's and Pocahontas' skin tones were made lighter, and Merida was given a narrower waist and a more voluminous hairstyle. Disney had to take some criticism for these changes because the company was accused of promoting stereotypical ideals.

Questions Upon Questions

At the latest, during a visit to Disney World – if not before – some questions will undoubtedly arise. Not about closing times, but rather questions about how such a world as the one created by Disney is actually possible. What are the tricks behind the camera? How does the company manage to provide magical moments again and again? Those with genuine interest – and a few dollars to spare – can have these questions answered by a specialist. A private conversation with Disney executives can be easily arranged through the "Dine with an Imagineer" project. Interested parties can meet studio employees over lunch and give free rein to all their questions.

Linguistic Geniuses

Every now and then, inventing a fictional language for a film is necessary. The creative mind behind the Atlantean from the Disney film *Atlantis – The Lost Empire* was also responsible for the popular Klingon in *Star Trek*. The inventor of both languages, Marc Okrand, also served as inspiration for the film's main character Milo, who is a linguist himself.

Royal Lineage

The Disney princesses have a very special status in the world of the media giant. But even the representatives of this special club show certain differences. This does not mean their appearance or character but rather the representation of their ancestry. You can tell a lot about the princesses by their clothing choice. For example, Cinderella, Belle, and Tiana wear opera gloves along with their pompous dresses, that is, gloves that reach almost to the elbow.

In contrast, Ariel, Merida, or Rapunzel will probably never be seen wearing such gloves. The reason: Only Disney princesses who achieve royal status by marrying a prince wear them. Born princesses, on the other hand, are depicted without gloves.

Secret Passages

How is it that Disney World employees actually turn up unseen exactly where they are supposed to be? The answer is an underground tunnel system. These secret tunnels are particularly advantageous for the disguised workers, as they must never appear in a park area where their characters do not belong. It is curious that, strictly speaking, the tunnels are not underground but located at ground level. Accordingly, the park above is actually on the 1st floor. The reason for this is Florida's high water table.

The Ice-Cold Queen

The plot of *Frozen* kept changing during the planning process. The most significant change, however, was that Elsa was originally intended to be the story's villain. The impetus for the change was not that those responsible did not like the plot, but a very special song in the film: *Let It Go*. The filmmakers liked it so much that they completely turned Elsa's story around. Whether the film would have been such a success if they had continued with the initial idea remains uncertain.

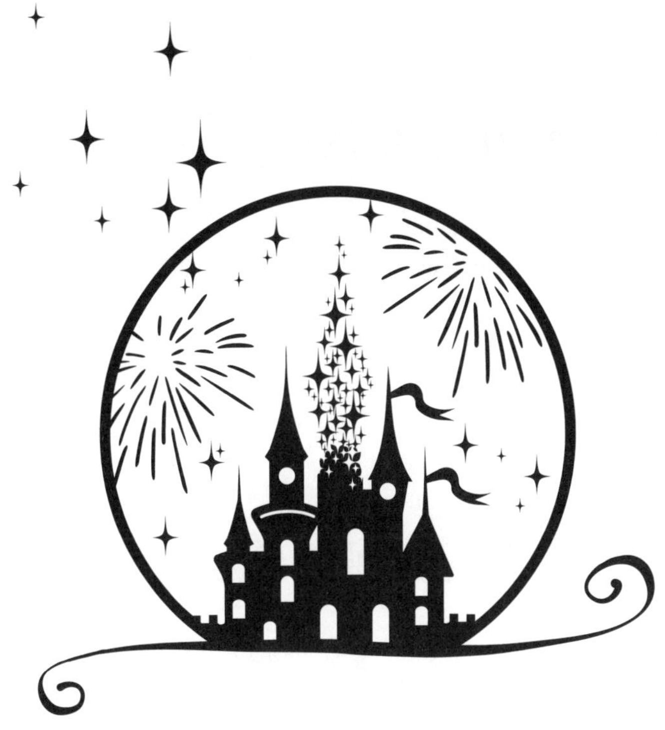

The prince from *Sleeping Beauty* is called Phillip. His name was probably inspired by a real royal: After all, it is the same name as the late Prince Phillip, husband to the former Queen Elizabeth II.

Hidden emaN

Disney is truly magical. This not only applies to the fairy-tale worlds that are created in its films but also quite literally. In the film *Fantasia*, the name of the magician is Yen Sid. If you read this name backward, you get Disney.

Life Writes the Stories

Leaving aside the legend of sea monsters and sea people, the film *Luca* is based on an actual incident. A man responsible behind the scenes of the film also grew up in a small coastal town in Italy, where a young troublemaker helped him gain confidence.

Who Lives Here?

The landmark of any Disney Park is the gigantic castle at the heart of the site. The castles themselves differ depending on the park. The castles' exterior and names are based on a specific Disney character. While Disneyland in Florida, for example, is adorned with the Cinderella Castle, the Sleeping Beauty Castle is in Paris.

A Hairy Affair

Blonde, long (very long) hair is the trademark of Disney princess Rapunzel. Based on the movie *Tangled*, her hair would have to reach a whopping 68 feet. On the scale, this head of hair would weigh about 20 pounds. Not so easy to lead an everyday life with such a mass. So maybe Rapunzel's choice to cut her hair shorter was simply a logistical decision.

Fox or Hare?

When planning a new film, the initial idea often looks very different from what eventually comes out. This also applied to the popular animated film *Zootopia*. The story mainly revolves around a bunny named Judy. During her adventures in the big city, she meets a fox called Nick Wilde, a crowd favorite but not the film's main character. Had the movie followed the original plan, things would have been different. Initially, the fox was meant to be the story's main protagonist. However, a test audience to whom the idea was pitched found it more interesting to elaborate on Judy's background story. Therefore, the original plan was scrapped, and the bunny was made the main character of the story.

Disney Times Differently

For many fans, becoming a Disney character is on the list of dreams they want to fulfill. For this purpose, they usually dig deep into their pockets and buy a costume of their chosen Disney character – quite expensive! Fortunately, however, it can also be done more cheaply. "Disney Bounding" shows how it works. The term refers to a movement in which fans use everyday objects and simple clothing to imitate the most popular Disney characters and recreate their costumes. The costumes then no longer refer only to the official costumes of the characters but also allow for reinterpretations of how the characters would dress in today's everyday life. This type of costume could be of particular interest for adult Disney fans since they are not allowed to enter the parks of the House of Mouse in complete Disney disguise. The responsible persons probably fear that one could confuse them with the workers of the park. Therefore, the almost-costume turns out to be a practical alternative.

A Singer for a Singer

The voice of pop singer Gazelle from the animated film *Zootopia* might sound familiar to some. None other than the singer Shakira takes on the role of the voice actress. In fact, the superstar could immediately identify with the role because the two have very similar character traits.

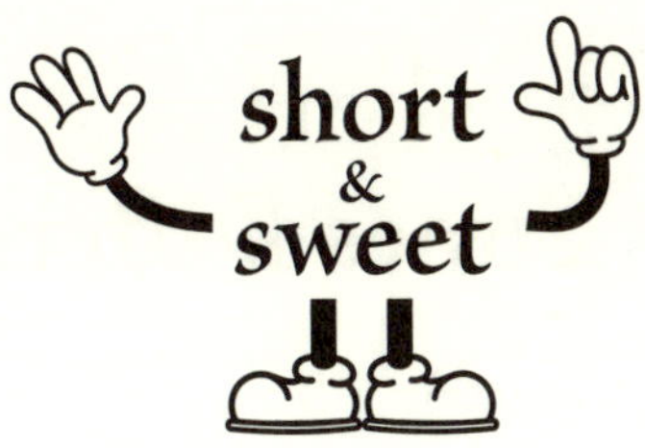

Despite being one of the most famous Disney movies, *Snow White and the Seven Dwarfs* never got a sequel.

The well-known song *Can You Feel The Love Tonight* from *The Lion King* was not originally intended to be sung by Simba and Nala. The initially chosen singers of the song were Timon and Pumbaa.

Ten special effects artists had to work for over a year to create the storm in *The Little Mermaid*, which whizzes by on screen in just about two minutes.

In Disney World, there is an area called Magic Kingdom. Among other things, a large oak tree has contributed to the park in a very special way. Over 500 of its acorns have populated the entire park area with trees.

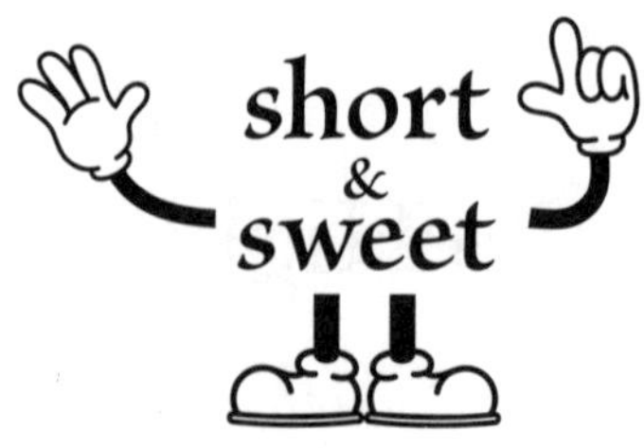

If you've always wanted to own your own Cinderella castle, you can fulfill that dream at Crystal Arts, a store on Main Street in Disneyland. The castle, consisting of over 28,000 Swarovski crystals, can be purchased there for "only" approx. 37,000 dollars.

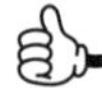

The opening of the Space Mountain area at Disneyland was even attended by real astronauts.

With more than 21 million liters of capacity, the Aquarium of the Seas at Disney's Epcot Park is one of the largest aquariums in the world.

The song *Part of Your World* was almost deleted from the final version of *The Little Mermaid*. In the end, however, it was decided to keep the song in the film.

The Ken doll in *Toy Story 3* is modeled after the 1988 Animal Lovin' Ken model.

Red for the Highborn

In times past, certain colors often stood for very special social classes. The color red, for example, was often associated with nobility or even the royal family. This fact does not refer only to a particular culture but is the same in many world regions. This is probably the reason why the color is considered high quality because in the past it was challenging to produce. Thus, only wealthy families could afford red-dyed clothing. Polynesian cultures and tribes also attributed the color to the royal class. Therefore, it's no wonder that Moana also often wears red in her film or is adorned with red feathers when she is performing her royal duties.

Special Agents at Sea

Fans of *Finding Nemo* may have been a little disappointed with a tiny detail in the *Finding Dory* sequel: The group of fish that Nemo met in the aquarium at the dentist's office barely appears in *Finding Dory.* The only scene in which the group appears is after the credits. They can still be seen in their dirty plastic bags, with which they had escaped from the aquarium in the first part. Initially, however, the whole thing was probably planned differently. In a deleted scene that didn't make it into the final film, the group is much more actively involved in the action. Here, Jacques and Peach try to use the coordinates of a ship that they infiltrate to find Dory.

Decoration for the Nation

Every year, on July 4, countless decorations and fireworks are brought out to mark the occasion. Although the next Independence Day was still several months away, there was another occasion where the decorations in the national colors were taken out, and the whole Disney World area was decorated with them. The reason for this, however, was not at all celebratory. One day earlier, on September 11, 2001, one of the greatest tragedies in the United States took place: the attack on the World Trade Center. Disney World was fully evacuated that day in just 30 minutes. It was feared that the park could also be a target of attack due to the high number of visitors, so it was decided to bring the guests to safety as soon as possible. After the tragic events, the park employees worked all night to offer the nation a glimmer of hope and a sign of solidarity. Disney World opened its doors the next day and presented itself in full Fourth of July decoration.

Left or Right?

Very few Disney princesses are left-handed. In fact, only three of them are known so far: Tiana, Mulan, and Raya. Mulan, however, cannot be clearly described as left-handed. Although she uses her left hand for archery, she holds her sword with her right. Therefore, she may also be ambidextrous.

Different Monsters

Monsters, Inc. is probably the greatest adventure of Mike and Sully. In the movie, the two monsters try to bring little Boo back into her world, and many things go wrong. Originally, the plot was planned quite differently. Initially, the story was supposed to revolve around a man instead of the monsters. Monsters were still supposed to appear – but in the role of the villains. In the story, the man was to be haunted by the monsters he had drawn as a child. They were to represent his fears, which he was to face gradually. In the end, however, this rather dark plot was replaced by the one we know today.

Wild Animal

The Beast from *Beauty and the Beast* is inspired by several animals. The legs and tail are modeled after a wolf, the head after a buffalo, the tusks mimic those of a wild boar, and the mane belongs to a lion. Even the eyebrows were inspired by an animal: They belong to a gorilla. Despite these many different aspects, the beast looks very coherent in its own way and overall resembles the physique of a bear.

Once Upon a Time...

The Disney Princesses are among the most popular characters in the Disney universe. Until 2005, the group included two characters who are no longer part of the official Disney Princesses. Both Esmeralda from *The Hunchback of Notre Dame* and Tinkerbell, made famous by *Peter Pan,* were initially also counted as Disney princesses.

Shoes for A Reason

Of course, bringing a film to the big screen takes quite a bit of time. Animated films are no exception. Many individual steps are involved, and every image of the film needs to be animated and brought to life. For animators, it's usually a fine line between the quality that needs to be delivered and having to meet deadlines. For this reason, they occasionally resort to little tricks to ease the workload. For the movie *Ratatouille,* such a trick was also used. Every single person in the film wears shoes at all times. Why? Animating the individual feet would have been too time-consuming, whereas the simple solution saved the people in charge a lot of time.

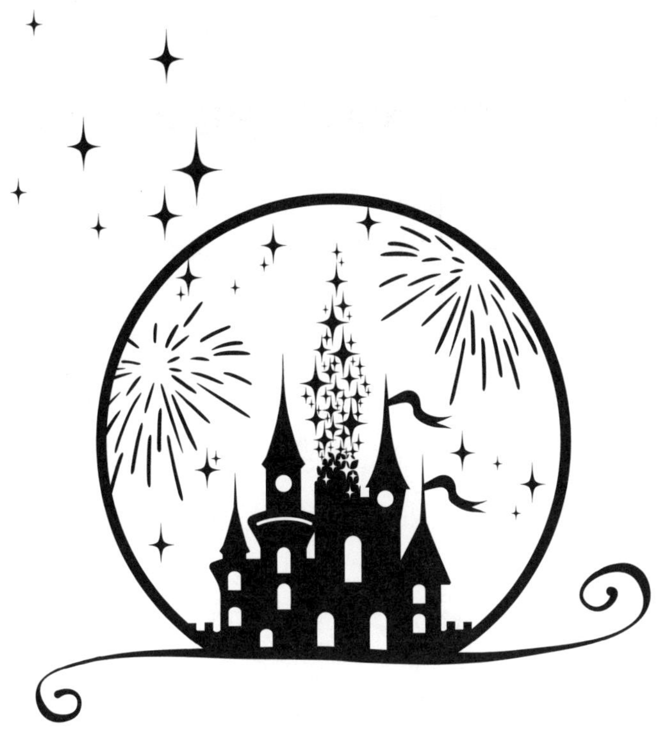

In Disney's Animal Kingdom, balloons and plastic straws are entirely forbidden. The rule is enforced to make sure the animals stay healthy and safe.

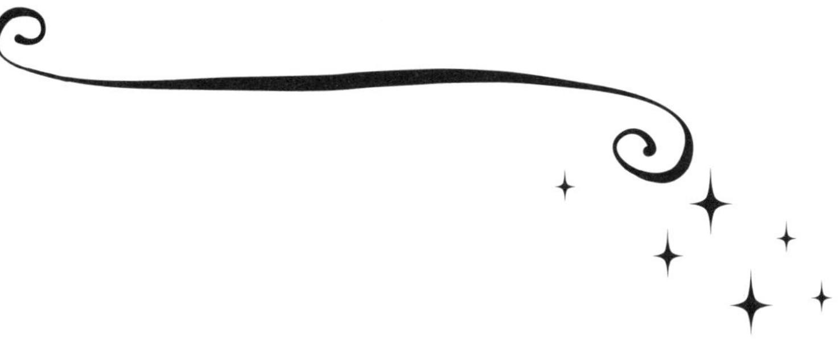

Please Do Not Imitate

After the release of the film *The Princess and the Frog*, there was an increase in children who had to be hospitalized because they had kissed a frog. Since some frogs and toads release incompatible or even toxic substances through their skin, children often had a health-related reaction. The idea of kissing a frog in the first place had probably come to the children from watching the film.

Disney on Fire!

If you imagine visiting Disney World, the day will probably be bursting with exciting attractions, numerous meetings with Disney characters, and lots of fun. The experience will probably end with a relaxing view of the Disney Castle, over which a massive fireworks display will shine. Wonderful! But to really guarantee such an experience, it takes a lot. If every guest wants to see fireworks during their visit alone, quite a lot of explosives are needed. No wonder that Disney World is one of the biggest buyers when it comes to fireworks. In fact, the park is the second-largest buyer of explosives in the United States. Only the American military surpasses its purchase figures.

Homemade Music

Tarzan is famous not only for its sweeping story or the film's accomplished animation but also for its soundtrack. Many of the songs heard in the film were composed and sung by Phil Collins. The song *Trashin' the Camp,* in which the scientists' camp is turned upside down, is also no exception. Here, the rock legend himself even created the sounds that occur when glasses or pots are banged.

Dream Job

Jumping into a chic costume, strolling through the park, and taking a photo here and there with excited fans – that's how many people imagine a job at the Disney Parks. In principle, that's not so wrong, but it takes a lot to get such a job. The employees are subject to strict rules. For example, they are not allowed to step out of their roles at any time and must always answer with the same level of knowledge as the character they are portraying. For instance, if you ask Snow White about the brand of her smartphone, you'll probably only get confused looks. Specific body measurements and the ability to perfectly imitate the signature of the respective character are also part of the employees' tasks.

Disney at Sea

If one fancies a vacation with Disney flair, places like Disneyland or Disney World usually come to mind first. But there are other ways to go about it. For example, if you'd rather go to the sea than a theme park, you can plan your next cruise with Disney. The House of Mouse maintains several ships and even its own island near the Bahamas, where Disney ports are located. The ships offer various tours worldwide, but one thing always remains the same: the entertainment value. After all, there's never a dull moment on a Disney ship. Concerts, comedy nights, musicals, and fireworks are just a few examples of the special features that a Disney cruise offers.

No Entry with Beard

In the early years, Disneyland had special rules regarding the dress code. In the 1960s, for example, employees and visitors were prohibited from wearing a beard. For Walt Disney, a beard did not fit into the image of a happy family since bearded people were considered hippies in the US at that time. The regulations were adapted and changed repeatedly so that nowadays, of course, beard wearers are also welcome in the theme park.

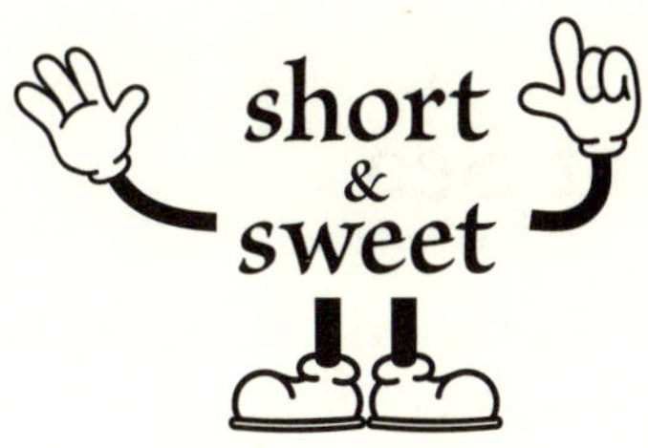

A roller coaster in the Disney Parks with a rock theme should have the right background music. Initially, the band U2 was chosen for this venture, but when they declined, Aerosmith was chosen.

The Disney animators always come up with little ideas to add subtle messages to the movies. For instance, such a detail can be found in *Aladdin*. The feather on his turban always falls into his face as soon as he lies.

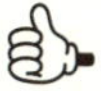

Thomas, John Smith's somewhat scatterbrained comrade-in-arms in *Pocahontas*, was voiced by none other than Christian Bale. The dubbing role definitely didn't harm the superstar's image.

Films can often have a particularly defining moment. For Paul McCartney, the film *Bambi* provided an eye-opener. The Disney classic convinced the singer that he would never approve of hunting and inspired him to become an animal rights activist.

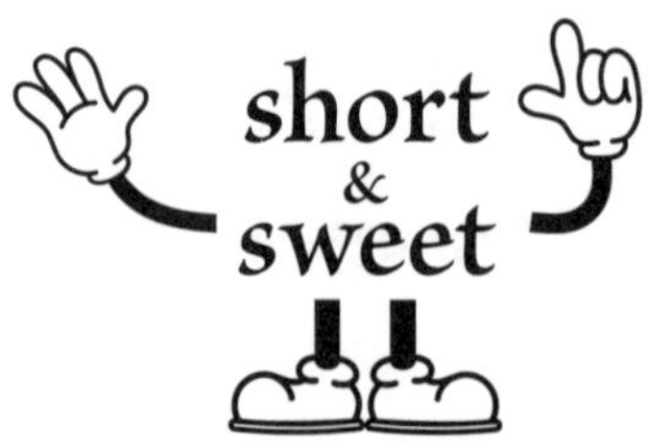

Instead of the animated version we know today, *Alice in Wonderland* was initially supposed to be produced as a live-action film. It was not until 60 years later that Disney dared to turn the cartoon into a live-action movie, with Johnny Depp as the Hatter.

Disney hired a snow expert to make the snow in *Frozen* look as realistic as possible.

Wayne Allwine, the voice actor of Mickey Mouse from 1977 to 2009, was married to the voice actress of Minnie Mouse. Not only on the screen a good team!

Most Pixar fans are probably familiar with the name Pizza Planet. The fictional company was originally to bear the name Pizza Putt, representing a combination of a mini-golf course and a pizzeria.

To Go, Please!

If you suddenly have a craving for popcorn on your way through the Disney Parks, it could be because of the smell. The Main Street area of Disneyland is artificially flooded with the scent of popcorn. According to those responsible, an experience is only complete when the sense of smell is also involved. But if you think popcorn is the only scent, you're wrong: Different aromas are used in other parts of the park.

Mercy for Coral

Probably one of the saddest scenes in the animated hit *Finding Nemo* can be seen right at the beginning of the film. A barracuda swims towards the reef and (most likely) attacks Nemo's mother Coral, as well as the eggs she had laid. While the exact whereabouts of Marlin's wife and her eggs remain unknown, the assumption is that the predatory fish has something to do with their disappearance. An original idea for the scene would have further reinforced this fact. The scene was initially intended to be more brutal. In a first draft, the creators planned for Coral to be seen disappearing into the mouth of the big fish. However, this detail was not included in the final version. Those responsible probably wanted to avoid the scene being too traumatic for a younger audience.

Look Closely

Just like the Disney princesses, the Disney villains count as a separate franchise. Like the princesses or other characters in the Disney universe, the villains have certain distinguishing features. For example, the colors black, purple, and red often play a role in their choice of clothing. When it comes to the eyes, it also becomes apparent who is the Disney villain. The villains often feature eye colors such as black, green, or even yellow. The colors have a purpose, of course. While yellow eyes are primarily found in the animal world with predators, the color green is associated with magic and witchcraft. However, these eye colors do not apply to all villains, and counterparts with other eye colors also appear repeatedly. Another peculiarity of the villains' eyes is that they usually do not reflect any light and are smaller than the heroes' eyes.

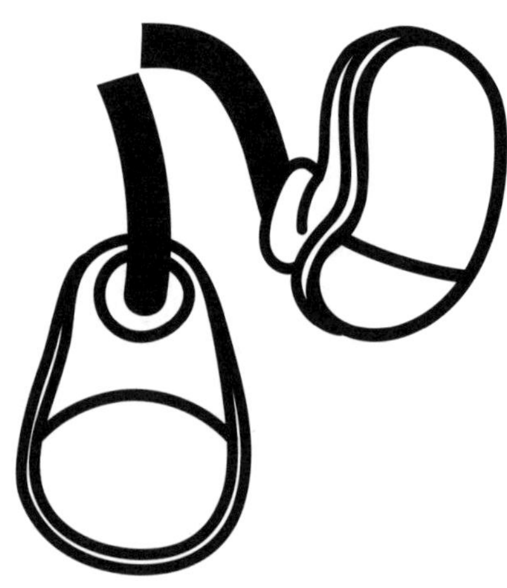

Listen Up!

In contrast to films shot with real people, an animated movie always needs individual actors to give the animated characters a voice. Usually, a female voice actor is cast for a female character. Sometimes, however, a female character's voice can also be dubbed by a man. This is what happened with the character Edna Mode from *The Incredibles*. Her voice was done by Brad Bird. However, she is not the first Pixar character to be portrayed as female but voiced by a man. The voice of Roz from *Monsters, Inc.* also comes from a man – Bob Peterson.

A Real Star Among the Stars

The Academy Award, also simply known as the Oscar, is one of the most coveted film prizes in the world. Actors, directors, and other film industry representatives are already pleased about a nomination for the award. To actually win the award then means a lot. However, for Disney founder Walt Disney, such an honor could almost have been nothing special anymore. He was nominated a total of 63 times during his lifetime and even after his death and won the award as many as 26 times. Until now, this record of awards remains unbroken.

Agent Disney

In the times of the Cold War, the USA was always vigilant. Not even the film industry was safe from investigations, and also the FBI got involved. They even turned to Disney founder Walt Disney, demanding his support. The film legend was supposed to inform if anything suspicious happened in Hollywood. Disney allegedly even signed a contract tying him to the FBI. What exactly was part of his services, however, remained a secret.

Long Becomes Short

The Second World War had an impact on just about everything. It also brought about changes in the film industry. For the Disney studio, the war meant, above all, a financial low phase. Some films that had been planned were canceled or heavily modified. This was also the case with a film adaptation of the story *The Legend of Sleepy Hollow.* Originally, it was planned to make a complete feature-length film out of it, but due to budget cuts, only a short film could be produced. Later, it appeared with the short movie based on Kenneth Grahame's *The Wind in the Willows* in the film *The Adventures of Ichabod and Mr. Toad.*

Not one Disney Park sells bubble gum. With this regulation, those responsible want to ensure the parks and their environment remain clean.

Unpleasant Discovery

In most cases, movie fans are happy to find small details in movies that most people would not notice. Occasionally, however, things are discovered that can cause problems later. In *The Rescuers*, for example, fans noticed the image of a naked woman in the background of a scene. After this became public, Disney had to recall over three million videocassettes, and the scene was changed for further releases.

Blue, Blue, Blue

Almost every Disney princess wears blue clothing at some point in her story. Sometimes blue is the primary color of the princess outfit, as in the case of Jasmine from *Aladdin*, and other times the color is only worn in a specific scene or section of the plot, like, for instance, Mulan during her final encounter with Shan Yu. Rapunzel, however, doesn't show up in a blue dress until her appearance in a TV series. The only exception to this rule so far is Moana. She doesn't wear blue clothes, but the color shows up in another detail: Her grandmother's necklace provides a blue accent to her outfit.

Hard-Fought Role

It's not unusual for world stars to be interested in the next Disney production, wanting to be actively involved. With the announcement of *The Princess and the Frog*, several stars entered the race for the voice-over role. Model Tyra Banks as well as singers Beyoncé and Alicia Keys are just a few names who were interested in the role of Tiana. Alicia Keys even auditioned three times for the lead role, while Beyoncé quietly hoped to be offered the part without auditioning. In the end, however, the contested spot went to actress Anika Noni Rose.

Not So Great Fairy Tale Castle

The famous Disney castle from the company's logo stands as a replica in the Disney Parks, looking fabulously large. But as is often the case, not everything in the parks is as it seems. Many buildings appear much bigger than they are. The reason for this is a special technique in facade design. For example, the height of Sleeping Beauty's castle in Disneyland Paris is emphasized using this technique. The stones of the castle wall are painted in such a way that they become smaller towards the top. From the visitor's perspective, this gives the impression that the building is much bigger than it actually is. In reality, it is "only" about 190 feet high.

Animated Food?

If you are strolling through the Epcot theme park in Florida and suddenly get hungry, sooner or later you will decide to stop at a restaurant. If the choice falls on the Sunshine Seasons or the Garden Grill, you can even enjoy special meals. What's so special about them? They are genuine Disney productions. In fact, some of the food used is grown and processed right in the park. While riding the Living with the Land attraction, you can learn about agriculture and the harvesting techniques the House of Mouse applies.

No Exceptions for Celebrities

In Disneyland, it is forbidden to film while going on a ride in some of the attractions. This rule exists mainly for the safety of the visitors. Maybe someone should have told director George Lucas. The *Star Wars* creator actually tried to film while on a *Star Wars* ride. However, when a park employee caught him in the act, he promptly wanted to expel him from the park. Whether the employee simply took his job very seriously or just didn't know whom he was trying to hold accountable is not known.

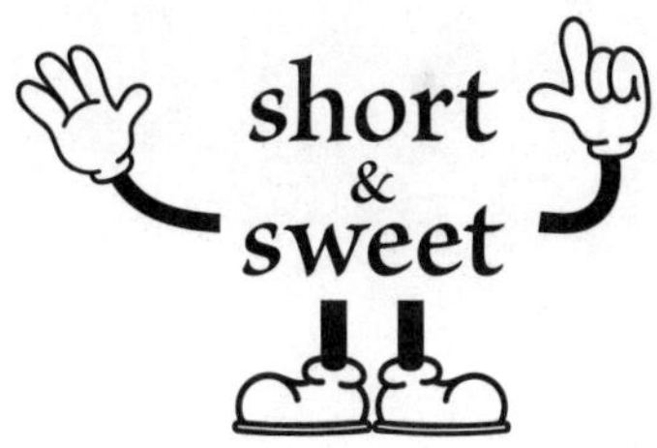

A reunion between Sully, Mike, and Boo was initially planned for the plot of the *Monsters, Inc.* sequel. In the film, the two monsters were supposed to venture into the world of humans, looking for their little friend from the first part. Instead, it was decided to do the complete opposite and present the story of the two monsters' past.

Snow White is still considered Disney's first big breakthrough. However, a sequel to the film never appeared – although it had been initially planned at one point.

Demigod Maui from the movie *Moana* is extremely popular with the audience. Apart from his tattoos, it is his head of hair that makes him stand out the most. Initially, however, the character was planned to be bald.

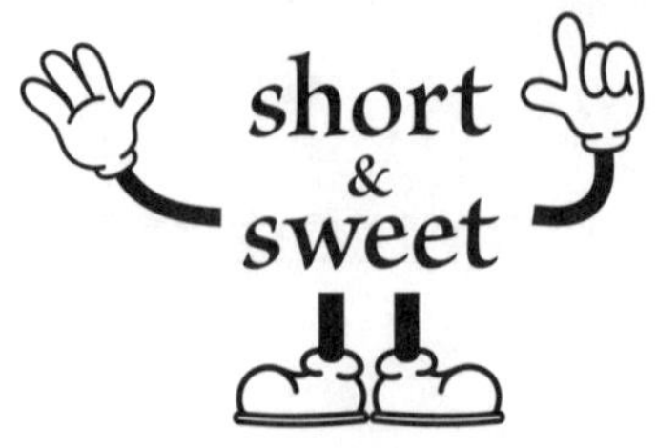

The film *The Incredibles* was originally supposed to be given a different title. It could almost have become known as *The Invincibles*.

The success of *Finding Nemo* ensured that demand for clownfish increased so rapidly that the species' abundance in some areas dropped dramatically.

Dopey from *Snow White and the Seven Dwarfs* does not speak a single word throughout the film. The character was originally not planned to be mute at all but rather quite talkative. In the end, he became so quiet because no suitable dubbing voice was found.

Disney World is not only synonymous with fun for the whole family; the parks are also considered the cleanest theme parks in all of America.

Fearful Environment

The fact that the Tower of Terror is meant to scare visitors of the Disney Parks in a certain way can already be guessed by the name. However, the atmosphere becomes even more intense when you are actually near the tower. Numerous screams then pierce through the air. Of course, many of them are real and coming from the visitors, but others are simply played from loudspeakers. To make the experience as authentic as possible, a few different screaming voices were recorded in advance and then played back near the tower.

Not the First Princess

Elsa is not the first Disney royal to be voiced by Idina Menzel. Menzel already became the dubbed voice of a princess in a Disney film when she lent her voice to Nancy from *Enchanted.* Although Nancy is not a born Disney princess, when she marries a prince towards the end of the film, she also becomes, strictly speaking, a princess in a Disney film.

The Cat Park

If you visit Disneyland in California, you might occasionally come across a cat, besides the numerous fans. However, the animal visitors are not on a short trip in the park. They live there. Especially after the park closes to visitors, the cats prowl the entire grounds. They are there because they help to keep the park free of pests and are regularly examined by veterinarians. The animals are also chipped – so they can really be considered part of the park's staff.

False Prejudices

Hyenas are evil, and lions are good. Viewers may have had this impression after watching *The Lion King*. After all, the film portrays the hyenas as relatively mindless henchmen of the villain Scar. In reality, however, hyenas are among the most successful hunters in Africa and are quite intelligent. They also drool much less than they appear to in the film. An expert of the predators sued Disney to save the honor of the hyenas and counteract the false image that the film paints of them. Others also joined the suit, but ultimately, it was unsuccessful.

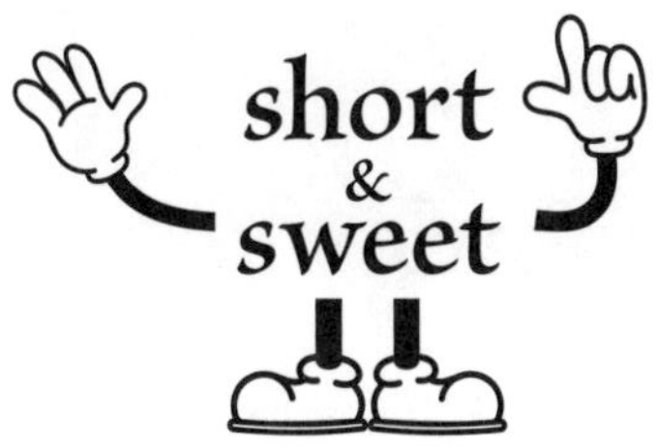

If you always thought that the English voices of Captain Hook and George Darling in *Peter Pan* were quite similar, you have good ears. In fact, both characters were spoken by the same voice actor.

The animation that Disney founder Walt Disney liked the most was the scene in *Cinderella* where her old clothes change into the pompous ball gown.

The staff that animated the movie *Frozen* used about 4,000 computers and still needed about 30 hours to complete a single frame. No wonder it took a full four years from the start of planning to the final film.

In Disneyland's first Snow White attraction, the princess was nowhere to be seen. Instead, the idea was to make visitors feel like they were slipping into the role themselves.

Visit From Space

Before the final plot of *Wall-E* was set, the idea of including aliens in the film was toyed with more than once. In one idea, Wall-E was supposed to encounter a spaceship full of aliens; in another, Eve was meant to be abducted by aliens. But since hardly anyone liked these ideas, they were quickly discarded.

Not a Good Vintage

A new Pixar film has been released in the US every year since 2005. One exception to this rule was in 2014 when no Pixar movie hit the screen. *The Good Dinosaur* was supposed to come out that year, but production was slightly delayed, so the film was not released until the following year.

Chaos with Age

Older viewers could almost have enjoyed a guest appearance by the *Golden Girls* characters in the film *Ralph Breaks the Internet*. In the end, the TV icons were not included, as it was feared that such an appearance would confuse younger viewers who were not familiar with the series from the 1980s.

Musical Vultures

Why do the vultures from *The Jungle Book* have such memorable hairstyles? These manes might even remind the older viewers of someone, and they wouldn't be wrong at all: The vultures were created in the image of the band The Beatles. The four band members were originally supposed to be heard in the film, but unfortunately, this plan was not realized due to scheduling conflict.

Of Clocks And Mice

The artist Salvador Dalí is undoubtedly known to most people for his surrealist depiction of melting clocks. Less well known, however, is that he also collaborated with film legend Walt Disney. The two created a project called *Destino* – a mix of dance and animation. The plot takes the viewer through the love story between the personified time and a human woman. In the process, the two also travel through different works by Dalí. The project started as early as 1945 but was paused briefly. However, it was not until 2003 that the work was completed by Dominique Monféry. Monféry had previously worked on many Disney films.

Happy End

Dory from *Finding Nemo* is brought to life by a very special voice actress: Ellen DeGeneres. The American host and comedian had a lot of fun with her role and jokingly complained for years that no sequel to the film was released. Maybe it was the jokes that made Pixar rethink? In 2016, the long-awaited second part (*Finding Dory*) was finally released, and Ellen could eventually slip back into her role.

The Shining Joy

In some scenes, a real glow emanates from the personified emotions shown in *Inside Out*. This glow is perfectly revealed in Joy and costs the makers of the film several months of work. After about eight months, however, when the Disney team had finally figured out how it was technically possible to make the figures glow, it also became clear that this approach would be very expensive. The specification to apply the glow to all emotions would have far exceeded the film's budget, so another solution was sought. Ultimately, they were happy to settle for just one character maintaining his glow throughout the film.

The King of the Tigers

At the zoo, many visitors like to spend time in front of the lions' enclosure. After all, the majestic animal is not called the king of beasts for no reason. Perhaps some people are reminded of the movie *The Lion King*. Especially, of course, when the animals raise their voices and roar loudly. But wait! This is precisely where discrepancies could arise. For the film, it was not the roar of lions that was recorded. Instead, the filmmakers turned to another predator: the tiger. Therefore, there are no lions to be heard in the movie but tigers. The decision was made in favor of the striped relative because tigers can roar louder than lions and this was more effective for the sound recordings.

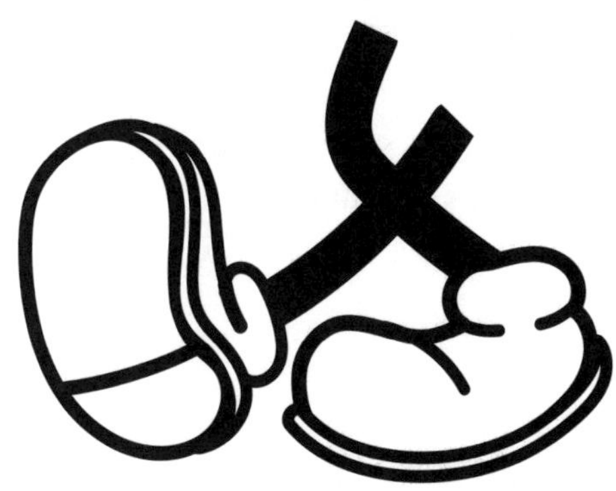

Fairy Tale Wedding

For all those who are looking for the perfect wedding location: How about the Cinderella Castle? In fact, you can get married there if you visit Disneyland. But not only the castle itself is available for the wedding. Some other aspects of the celebration can also be kept completely in the style of *Cinderella*. For example, a ride in Cinderella's carriage can be taken, Disney characters can be encountered at the celebration, and a huge fireworks display can be arranged. If this is not a fairy tale wedding...

Lieutenant Donald

The Second World War had an impact on pretty much every aspect of life. The film industry was no exception. Some production companies included the topic in their works or even actively tried to draw attention to it. So did media giant Disney. In the early 1940s, the company devoted itself to several projects intended to promote patriotism and confidence and were even used in the U.S. Army for training purposes. Even the classic Disney characters appeared in such films. For example, Donald Duck joins the army in the film *Donald in Uniform*.

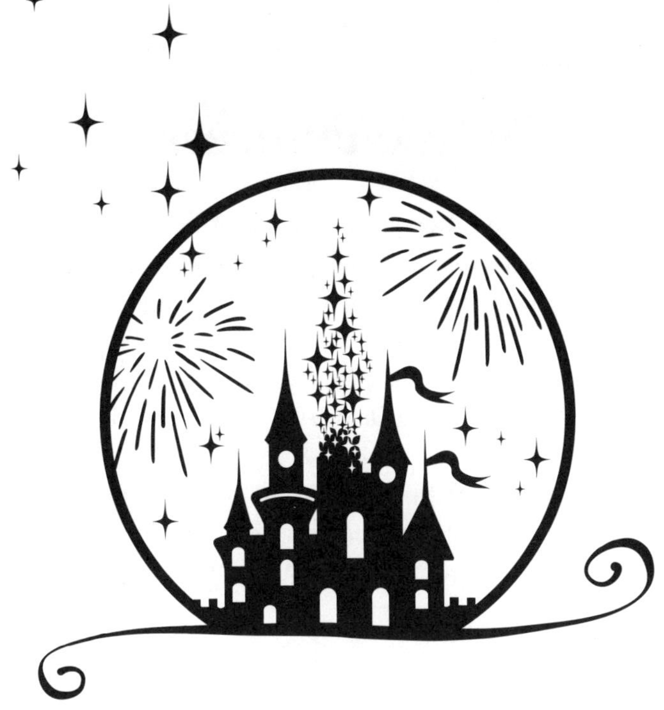

For over two years, Walt Disney held the sole right for animated films in color in the US. During that time, Disney held the patent for the so-called Technicolor technique, enabling Disney to produce color animated films.

The Unique Princess

Merida is an exception among Disney princesses regarding several categories. Probably the most critical difference to the other princesses: Strictly speaking, Merida is not a Disney princess but a Pixar princess. However, since Pixar is a subsidiary of the House of Mouse, she can still be counted among the Disney princesses. Merida also differs from the other princesses in terms of her family. She is a princess with brothers instead of (step)sisters. Furthermore, most other princesses in their respective movies have a romantic component. Merida, however, seems to be happiest alone.

A Close Call!

It wouldn't have taken much, and *Toy Story 2* might have never been released. The version that is known today was almost destroyed. The work of numerous hours the animators had already invested in the project over several months was deleted due to a small mistake. Fortunately, the material was saved. An employee found a copy on her home computer, which she had saved while working from home.

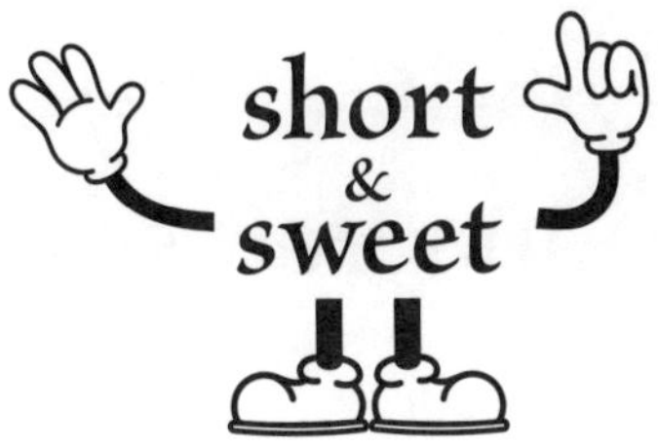

The second part of *Aladdin* was never shown in theaters but was produced directly as a home video on VHS tape. This made *The Return of Jafar* the first direct-to-video animated film in the US.

In initial character concepts, Elsa from *Frozen* was still depicted with short, dark hair.

Walt Disney may have had a special bond with the character Peter Pan. He played the boy who didn't want to grow up in a theater production at his school.

Initially, the film about the wooden boy Pinocchio didn't include the cricket Jiminy. The character was only added to the script later when Walt Disney found that Pinocchio needed a companion.

Rumor has it that real bones were partly used for the music in *Coco*.

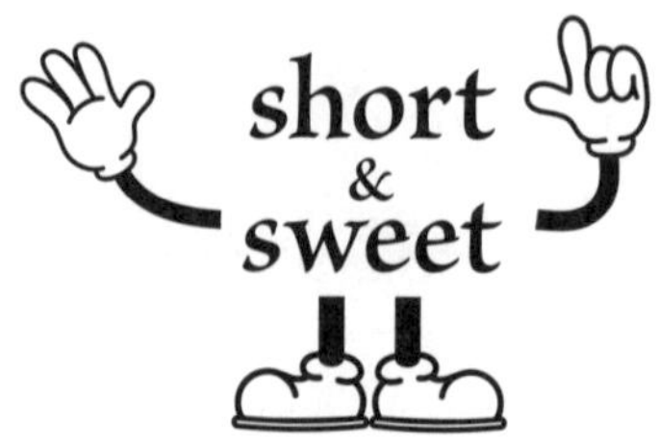

The spaceship simulation Mission Space at Epcot feels so real that some visitors may suffer from motion sickness.
For this reason, spit bags are also distributed at the attraction.

Anyone who thinks that women change their clothes more often than men will be proven wrong in *Toy Story 3*. Ken wears no fewer than 21 different outfits in the film.

To make the sparkle of Tinkerbell in *Peter Pan* recognizable on the soundtrack, those responsible did not use bells or anything similar but created the sounds with aluminum foil.

If you don't like the restaurants and snack stands inside the Disney Parks, you should take a look at the Walt Disney World app. There, a secret menu can be accessed at many locations, offering extraordinary dishes that change regularly and do not appear on the conventional menu.

Effective Test Run

How do you find the best place for trash cans in a theme park? Walt Disney had a simple solution: He tested himself where they should most plausibly be placed. This is how it happened that a trash can was placed exactly 25 steps away from the snack stand of a hot dog store. It was exactly the distance Walt Disney needed from the stand to eat a hot dog. Thus, the trash can was perfectly positioned to immediately dispose of the leftover garbage.

The Main Thing Is to Look Real!

You're in the middle of a tour of a Disney Park, when you suddenly have to go to the bathroom. Usually, that's not a problem since there are restrooms available in the parks. With one exception: Near Liberty Square in Disney World, visitors will search in vain for a quiet restroom. On the other hand, history buffs will almost be pleased by this fact. After all, there are no restrooms here since the square was meant to be depicted as historically authentic as possible. Toilets as we know them today simply did not exist back then.

Magical Children

Not only are there numerous rumors around the Disney Parks themselves, but there is also much to speculate about its visitors. For example, it is rumored that at least three children have been born in Disneyland so far. This assumption leads to speculation about the possible advantages of such a birthplace. For a long time, it was said that children born in Disneyland would receive free admission to the park for life. Disney, however, denied this statement and clarified that there is no such privilege. Another rumor claims that children born in the park invariably bear the names of Disney characters. Whether this is true, however, is not substantiated.

Talking Dogs

It's not that easy to make a dog talk believably. After all, there is no real-life model that the animators could have used as a guide. For this reason, they used a simple mirror and their own facial features to portray the dogs in *Lady and the Tramp*. They then tried to transfer the subtle changes that resulted from speaking or certain facial expressions to the dogs' designs. The aim was to make the dogs look more realistic.

Successful Lunch

There are days when things just don't go well. Whether it's at school or at work, sometimes you just can't concentrate properly. On other days, ideas just bubble up to make the day a success. Pixar employees had one such day in 1994. Over a single lunch, they came up with ideas for four films: *Monsters, Inc.*, *Finding Nemo*, *A Bug's Life*, and *Wall-E*. Naturally, the ideas for the movies were not fully developed then, but a big step for the future was taken.

Random Breakthrough

Disney employees are always pushing the limits to give fans an unforgettable experience. They conduct extensive research before each film project to ensure this. But even after the project is finished, the research does not stop. Scientists from Disney's Animal Kingdom continued their studies on elephants after the success of *Dumbo*. The Disney representatives happened to make an extraordinary discovery on one of their trips to Africa. They were able to achieve an extensive study of the elephants' communication, in which a completely new phenomenon was discovered: Elephants have a very specific call to warn each other about bees.

Strong Female

Patcha's wife, Chicha, from *The Emperor's New Groove,* takes on a special role among Disney women. Most Disney films do without a mother role at all. Chicha, however, is one of the few Disney mothers who not only appears in the movie but is also a recurring presence throughout the plot. She is also the first animated Disney character to be shown pregnant.

Witching Hour

Unfortunately, sometimes things go wrong in the process of building a theme park or individual attractions. This was also the case during the construction of the Pirates of the Caribbean ride at Disney World. Regretfully, a worker died in the process and has since been the cause of ghost rumors in the park. A small ritual has even developed among the remaining employees: Every evening, when the park closes its doors, the employees say goodbye to their deceased colleague and wish him a good night. There is a superstition among the employees that this protects them from possible further accidents.

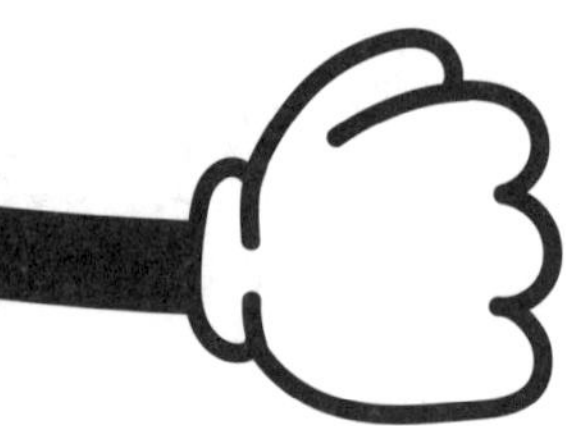

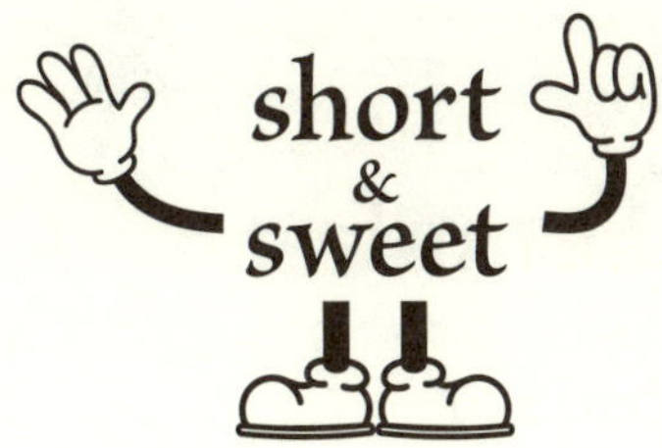

In contrast to the stereotype of the damsel in distress, in *The Little Mermaid* it is not the girl who is saved by the prince, but the prince by the girl. This makes the film the first among the Disney princess films to turn the tables.

When creating the character Cruella de Vil from *101 Dalmatians*, the filmmakers were partly inspired by the late actress Tallulah Bankhead.

If the son of one of the animators who worked on *Tarzan* hadn't loved skateboarding so much, Disney fans might have met a very different Tarzan. Instead of just swinging through the trees, Tarzan almost "skates" across the branches because his son inspired the employee.

For Aladdin's grin and some of his facial features, the animators drew inspiration from the actor Tom Cruise.

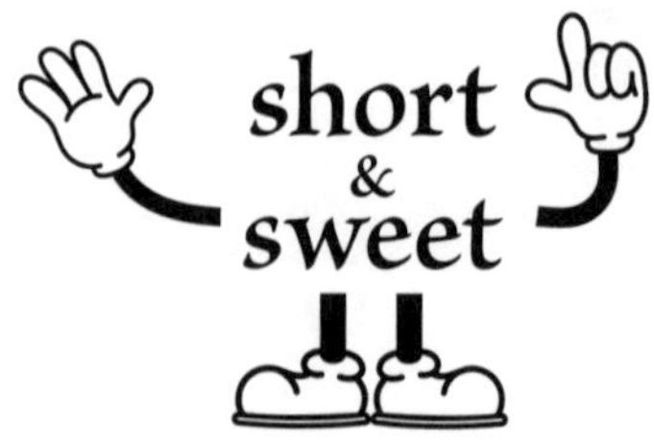

To achieve the perfect out-of-breath voice in *The Incredibles*, Dashiell "Dash" Parr's voice actor, Spencer Fox, ran several laps around the studio lot.

There are more than 330 official Disney Stores worldwide. The largest is located in Shanghai, China.

The Disney Parks have a strict no-dating rule. Thus, colleagues are prohibited from entering into a relationship beyond friendship.

Robin Williams did so many recordings for his role as the Genie in *Aladdin* that the makers ended up with several hours of audio material. Therefore, it wasn't easy to choose the best recordings.

Pixar fans might recognize the tree under which Ellie and Carl have a picnic in *Up*. It's the same tree where many scenes of *A Bug's Life* take place.

Christmas Transformation

String lights, garlands, and ornaments on the Christmas tree. For many, this is what the ideal Christmas decoration looks like. The Disney Parks, of course, always go the extra mile in terms of decoration. More precisely, a whole 150 truckloads go the extra mile. The Disney World grounds are thus transformed into a veritable winter wonderland every year. Over 3,000 Christmas trees are placed in the parks each year. While everyone else would have to worry about the electricity bill with many lights and illuminated signs, Disney takes a relaxed view. After all, the park produces its own electricity.

Cost Wars

At the end of the 1970s, science fiction films were very popular. No wonder since *Star Wars* had broken several records in 1977. Disney also wanted to profit from this trend. Since *Star Wars* was not yet part of the House of Mouse, Disney worked on its own live-action film set in outer space. The 1979 film *The Black Hole* turned out to be a total failure. Although the science fiction adventure had twice the budget of the first *Star Wars* film, at around 20 million dollars, and was technically impressive, it only brought in barely half of its production costs.

Mickey Mouse Is Not Real?!

Shocking but true: Mickey Mouse is not like other mice. Mickey can talk, wears clothes, is bigger than a cup, and generally appears rather human. However, Mickey lacks one particular human characteristic. Despite the many similarities, Mickey has only four fingers instead of five. The background: Many comic characters of the 1930s have only four fingers. It was much easier for the artists to draw a character with only four fingers per hand. So, the middle finger was omitted. Although drawing all five fingers nowadays would be easier, new figures are still usually done with only four fingers per hand.

A Beautiful Witch

In most depictions – especially when they date back a few years – witches are shown as ugly older women. Comic artist Carl Barks probably wanted to put an end to this when he created the Duckburg character Magica De Spell. The enchanting antagonist that Scrooge McDuck encounters a couple of times definitely can't be described as old or ugly. Barks drew inspiration for the creation from two Italian actresses and the character Morticia Addams from *The Addams Family.* Certain similarities can be identified without question.

Part of the Pride

Simba and Nala may not be the only lion cubs featured in *The Lion King*, but they are the only ones who play a role in the plot. In the early script versions, however, things were quite different. There, a little lion named Mheetu also appeared – Nala's brother. Simba was even supposed to save him from the panicked herd in the course of the story, but in the end, the character was emitted entirely.

Waited Too Long

When a film is produced over several years, it can entail a number of difficulties. One problem is that the dubbing actors might become too old over time. This was the case with the work on *The Sword in the Stone*, where the initially intended voice actor who was to speak the young Arthur had to be recast. At the time of recording, the young man's voice had already changed, which resulted in a different voice. The director's two sons stepped in as dubbing actors at short notice.

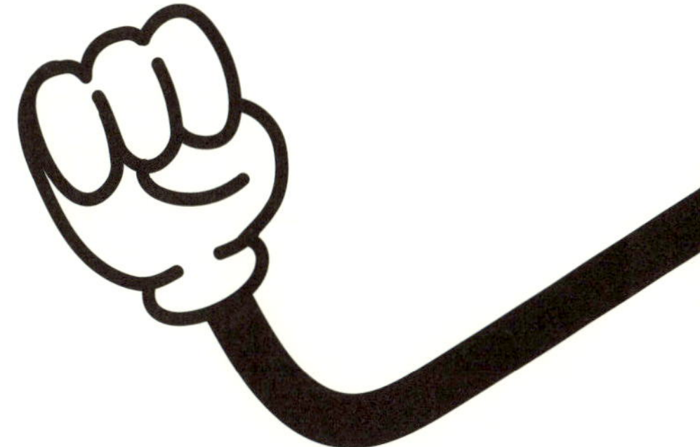

A Difficult Relationship

In fairy tales, and thus also in their Disney film adaptations, the evil stepmother often takes on the role of the villain. In *The Little Mermaid*, however, it is the sea witch Ursula, who is not related to Ariel, but who nevertheless plays an evil trick on her. In an earlier version of the plot, this was different. There, Ursula was supposed to be introduced as Triton's sister. Thus, she would have been Ariel's aunt.

Invented Language

Some fans of *Snow White and the Seven Dwarfs* were no doubt confused when they saw the spelling of the title. While the title itself is not unusual, another spelling for "dwarfs" has become established: "dwarves." While the first is the official spelling of the title and also the grammatically correct variant, "dwarves" is perhaps even more commonly used these days, which is why some Disney fans might be surprised at the title today. The reason for the change is J. R. R. Tolkien, who used the "new" spelling for his book series *The Lord of the Rings*. It has become so ingrained that many people consider it correct and it has been recognized in the canon, but grammatically only "dwarfs" is correct.

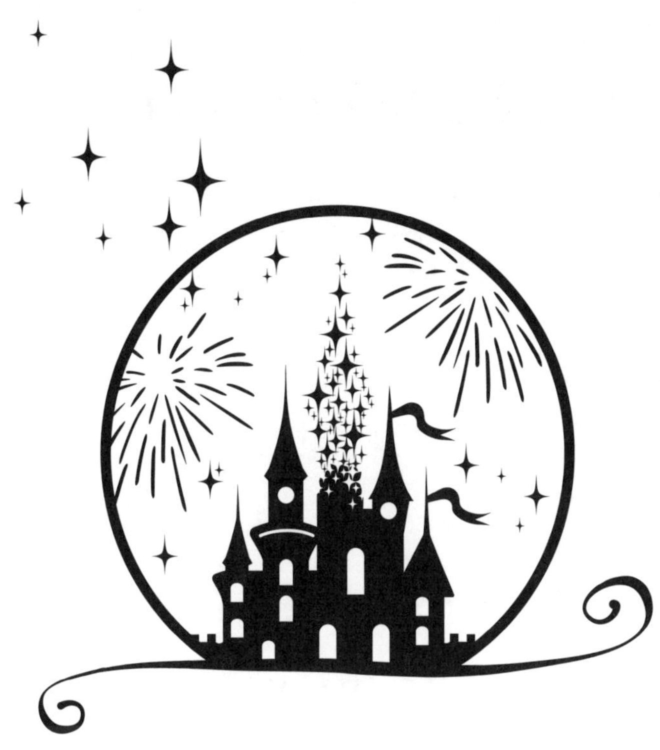

Aurora from *Sleeping Beauty* is probably the most silent Disney princess of all. She only has about 18 lines in her movie.

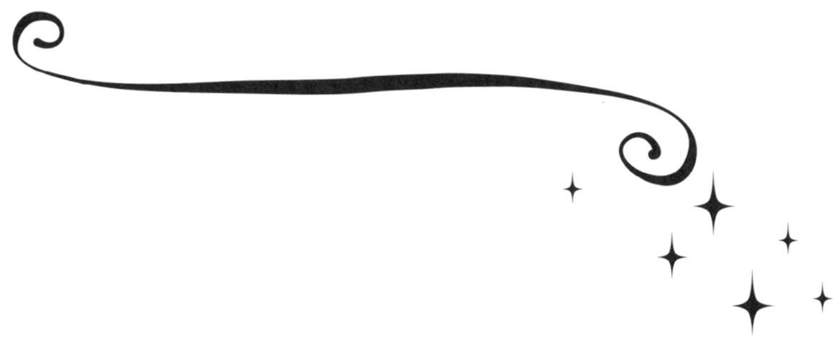

Special Opening Hours

If you've always wanted to experience a Disney Park without the usual crowds, you can do so. However, you must act quickly and dig deeper into your pockets. The so-called "Disney After Hours" tickets cost around 130 dollars each and are limited to 5,000 visitors. With these special tickets, visitors can stay in the park after the regular closing times and experience it differently.

Big Day for Little Performers

The fact that little Boo in *Monsters, Inc.* never seems to stand still is also evident in the way she speaks. Her voice sounds almost a little out of breath. No wonder: dubbing artist Mary Gibbs found it extremely difficult to stand still during her recordings. But that's understandable since she was excited about working at the same workplace as her father. He, in turn, works as a story artist at Pixar. After her portrayal of Boo, Mary did not voice any other roles at Disney, but some of her outtakes from the film were used in *Inside Out*.

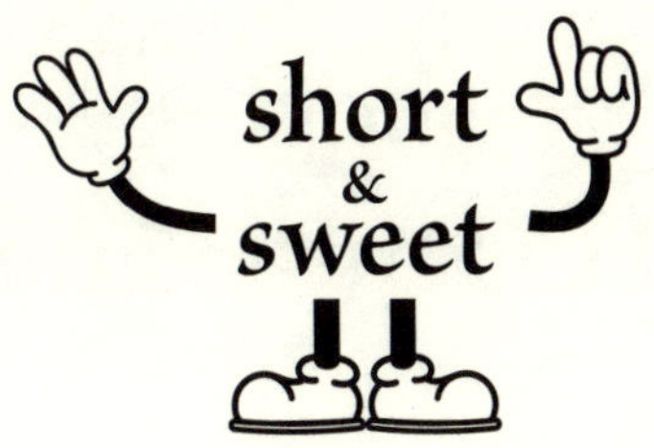

Lovers of action movies might have felt transported back to their childhood while watching *Transformers.* The reason: Optimus Prime's dubbing voice is the same one that voiced Eeyore the donkey in *Winnie the Pooh.*

Disney Channel Original Movies, such as *High School Musical, Camp Rock,* or *The Descendants* series, are usually filmed in just three months.

As with many other films, the plot of *Cars* was originally planned quite differently. Initially, the story was supposed to revolve around a three-wheeled car model that everyone was supposed to make fun of.

Certain items are prohibited in Disney Parks. These include pogo sticks, scooters, and inline skates.

Ariel is the Disney princess who sings the most songs in her film.

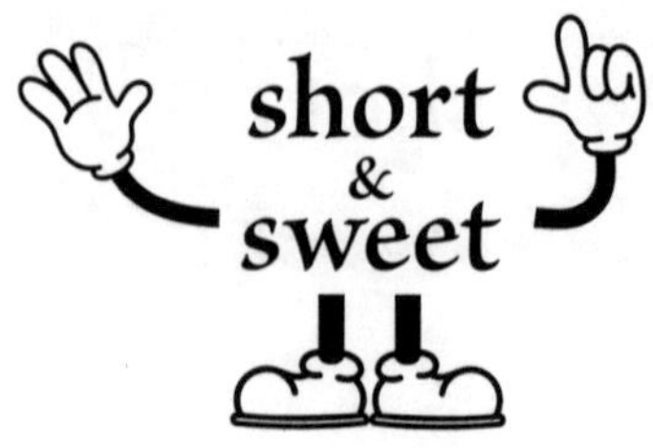

In order to provide the animators with a lifelike model to design Sven the reindeer for *Frozen*, the studio was visited by a real reindeer.

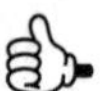

Beauty and the Beast was the first animated film ever to be nominated for the Oscar category "Best Picture." Although the film did not win the award, it was honored with the Academy Award for "Best Score" and "Best Song."

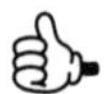

A "Disney vault" is located in Glendale, California. This is where all film materials and props are stored.

Lilo & Stitch is the first animated film that is not a short but a full-length feature film set exclusively in Hawaii.

The plot of *Frozen* is loosely based on the fairy tale *The Snow Queen* by Hans Christian Anderson.

The Federation of Sisters

What is it actually like to have a sister? Are there any special feelings or events that occur equally for all sisters? Disney employees must have asked themselves questions like these when planning the animated hit *Frozen*. To determine how it exactly feels to have a sister, Disney called a "Sisters Summit" to address such questions. According to those responsible, the summit was a complete success and helped the creators bring the story to the big screen.

Sharks Among Themselves

Some film greats even manage to appear in other films besides their own. They are often mentioned in passing, and sometimes the characters themselves appear in a guest role. Animated films are no exception. In *Finding Nemo*, for example, reference is made to an actual cinema legend: Bruce. The name of the shark who has sworn off eating fish is already well known from another film. But you're mistaken if you think of Bruce Wayne, Bruce Lee, or Bruce Banner. The shark's name is based on one of his fellow sharks – albeit not a real one. We are talking about the shark model that was used in *Jaws*. Among the film crew of that time, the replica was also known by the name Bruce.

Easter Eggs from the Future

It's no secret that Pixar repeatedly incorporates references from its films into other movies. But most people are unaware that these references can predict the future. For example, *Onward* features an album by musician Dorothea Williams. However, *Soul*, the film in which the musician first appears as a character, was only released several months after *Onward*.

Little Big Elephant

Can a film with just over an hour of running time succeed? The answer is yes, as is proven by *Dumbo*. Disney tells the story of the little elephant with big ears in no more than 64 minutes. This makes the feature film the shortest in the Disney portfolio – except for the short films, of course. The fact that the film was meant to be so short was not supported by many employees at the time. They feared that a movie this brief would not go down well with the audience. However, Walt Disney proved them wrong: He insisted on not artificially dragging out the film and ruining it. A good decision, considering that the film even won an Oscar. By the way, the film's remake from 2019 has almost twice the original's running time.

Success from the Sea

When planning a new film project, those responsible naturally always hope for success. Even if the resulting film is great in their opinion, it must also convince the audience. Unfortunately, this was not the case with *Sleeping Beauty*. In fact, the film was an absolute flop. Perhaps it was also unsuccessful because three different directors worked on the film during the eight years of production. Fearing that any other princess film might also not go down well with audiences, such productions were put on hold for a long period. It wasn't until 1989, 30 years later, that a new Disney princess movie, *The Little Mermaid*, hit theaters. This time it was a complete success and proved that Disney princess films can indeed be very popular.

The Garbage Planet

In *Wall-E*, it is the task of the little robot with the same name to clean the earth of the trash left behind by humans. Therefore, the film's title was initially supposed to be *Trash Planet*. The plot was also meant to be different in the beginning. Wall-E was to meet aliens and lead a revolution. During planning, however, this idea was discarded, and the now-known version of the film slowly took shape.

The Perfect Height

At first glance, the buildings of the Disney Parks appear huge to most. However, the majority of the buildings were designed not to exceed a certain height. Therefore, the Hollywood Tower of Terror or the Everest Expedition are "only" 199 feet high. The reason for this height is actually quite logical. From a height of 200 feet, structures in the US would have to be equipped with flashing red lights in order to alert airplanes and helicopters to the obstacle. To avoid this regulation, it was decided to use smaller structures.

Too Many Ideas, too Little Film

Sometimes there can be too many ideas for only one film. Since not all of these ideas can be realized in a single movie, some of them are simply postponed and used in a sequel instead. Even for *Toy Story*, many more scenes were initially planned, but then a couple of them were included in *Toy Story 2*. For instance, viewers could have already experienced the garage sale, Woody's nightmare, or Buzz's cartoon in the first part.

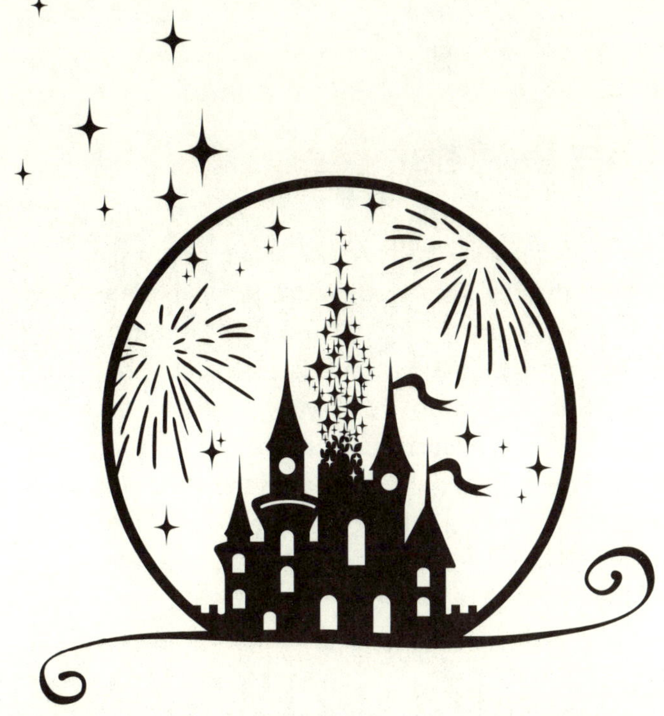

No one would have expected the song *Let It Go* from *Frozen* to become such a success. It was the first Disney song to have made it to the Top 10 in the US since 1995. Even more surprising is that the song was written in only one day.

A Good Excuse

The fact that the dance scenes in *Sleeping Beauty* and *Beauty and the Beast* follow the same movements is quickly noticed when comparing the two films. Unlike other reused animations, in this case, an existing work was not used for the sake of money. The filmmakers were simply under too much time pressure while working on *Beauty and the Beast*. So, they used the older animation to save time and meet their deadline.

Unwanted Visit

Disney World is one of the most popular destinations in Florida. Every year, the park counts thousands of visitors, some of whom are not at all intentional. Of course, this is not about Disney fans enjoying the attractions but about animal guests. Florida is known to be home to many alligators due to its swamps. But the Everglades is not the only region where the giant reptiles can be found. The animals also make themselves at home in Disney World from time to time. They are particularly fond of the Seven Seas Lagoon attraction. Time and again, visitors report seeing alligators there.

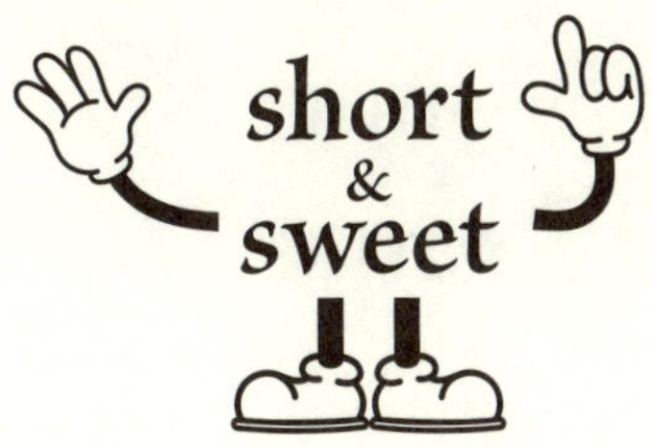

The Mickey Mouse hat, with which anyone can quickly give themselves two mouse ears, was originally designed for the short film *The Karnival Kid.* Nowadays, it can be bought as a souvenir in the Disney Parks.

In comparison to all Disney princesses, Rapunzel has the biggest eyes.

The hotels at Disney World have a total of around 30,000 rooms. To sleep in all of them, you would need about 68 years.

It's hard to imagine the Disney classic *Pocahontas* without Grandmother Willow. It is all the more shocking that the character did not even appear in the script's first version. Instead, Pocahontas was supposed to seek advice from another figure: a river spirit.

Although Disney's mascot is a mouse, Walt Disney is said to have been panicky about the little rodents.

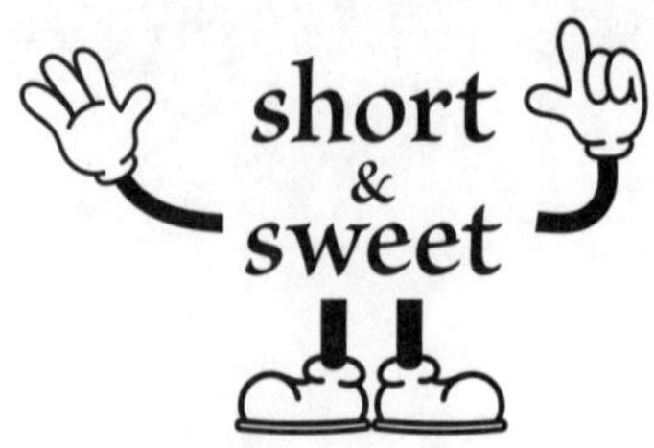

Mickey & Minnie Mouse, Donald & Daisy Duck, and Pluto & Goofy form the so-called Sensational Six and are among the most famous Disney characters of all time.

If you think everything at Disney is just for show, you're wrong: Even the drawbridge of Sleeping Beauty's castle at Disneyland actually works.

Although many fans of *The Lion King* think Rafiki is a baboon, he is actually a cross between a baboon and a mandrill.

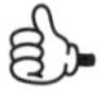

The only Disney princess with a tattoo is Pocahontas.

The singing voice of Disney princesses Mulan and Jasmine is the same. The songs of both characters were sung by Lea Salonga.

Family Matters

Disney's *Frozen* is probably one of the most famous and popular Disney films of recent years. Not only the story itself but also the film music has contributed majorly to this success. Perhaps the music fits so well because the people who are responsible for it, Kristen Anderson-Lopez and Robert Lopez, are married and therefore very close even outside of work. The songwriters also have two daughters, which helped them to have a better understanding of the sisterly bond that is an essential part of the film's plot. One of their daughters, Katie, even appears in the movie. She sings the first verse of the song *Do You Want to Build a Snowman.*

In the Jungle of India

The story of Mowgli has been repeatedly told. The plot was originally based on the anthology *The Jungle Book* from 1894. In this original version, Mowgli's story is somewhat different from the film adaptations. One big difference, for example, is how Mowgli comes to live with his foster parents – the wolves. While in the Disney animated film, Mowgli is brought by panther Bagheera to the wolf family that eventually raises him, in the original book Mowgli himself escapes to the wolf's den in order to escape the tiger, Shere Khan.

Old Friends

Waiting in line at the attractions in the Disney Parks should never be boring. At least, that's what those responsible seem to have thought. Sometimes hidden messages can be detected in the loudspeaker announcements of the employees. This is also the case with the Star Tours roller coaster at Disneyland. An announcement to a certain Mr. Egroeg Sacul can be picked up there. If you look closer at the name, you will quickly realize who it really is. If you read it backward, you get the name of *Star Wars* creator George Lucas. Even before Disney took over Lucasfilm, the Hollywood star had a connection with Disneyland. He was even present at its opening when he was eleven years old.

International Princess

The animated hit *Raya and The Last Dragon* incorporates several different cultures into the story. Raya herself even shows different influences in her fighting style. It is reminiscent of the Indonesian Pencak Silat, but she also uses two sticks like in the Filipino Kali. Even her name has its origin from two different languages. "Raya" is translated as "to celebrate" in both languages of Malaysia and Indonesia.

The Success of a Family

Fans of the Pixar film *The Incredibles* had to wait for 14 years. In 2018, the long-awaited sequel to the film finally hit theaters. But it wasn't just fans who benefited from this decision. *The Incredibles 2* generated over 1.2 billion dollars on the international market. This means that the superheroes even surpassed the previous record of over one billion dollars set by *Toy Story 3*. *The Incredibles 2* has since become the most financially successful Pixar film.

Dangerous Content?

Nowadays, movies have different ratings, especially in terms of age requirements. Disney films are also repeatedly assessed and given the appropriate ratings. The first PG rating for a Disney princess movie, meaning that it should only be watched by children accompanied by their parents, was given to the film *Tangled*. While it was the first princess film to receive this rating in the US, it was not the first animated Disney film ever to receive this rating. *The Black Cauldron* from 1985 was also given the PG label.

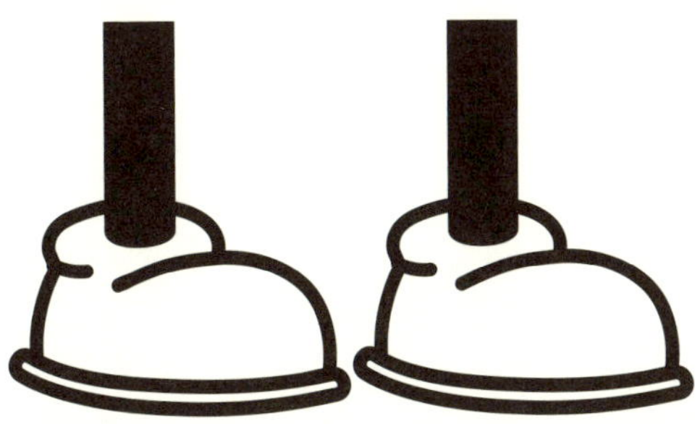

The Mute Robot

For 18 months, the filmmakers behind the Pixar movie *Wall-E* studied early silent films. Above all, films with Buster Keaton or Charlie Chaplin were watched over lunch. The reason: Those responsible were trying to find inspiration for the first half of their movie. Since Wall-E is alone on Earth at first and can't really talk yet, those responsible had to get a new take on telling the story without much dialogue. The fact that they drew on the well-known silent films of the two great filmmakers was definitely a smart move.

The Agony of Choice

When several films are produced simultaneously, it is unavoidable that employees are naturally assigned to a specific project and cannot work on several productions. When *Pocahontas* was made at the same time as *The Lion King*, the animators fought over who was allowed to work on which project. Surprisingly, it was believed at the time that *Pocahontas* would be the more successful film, which is why many of the staff wanted to be on the designated team. Only a few people at the time suspected that *The Lion King* would ultimately be even more popular.

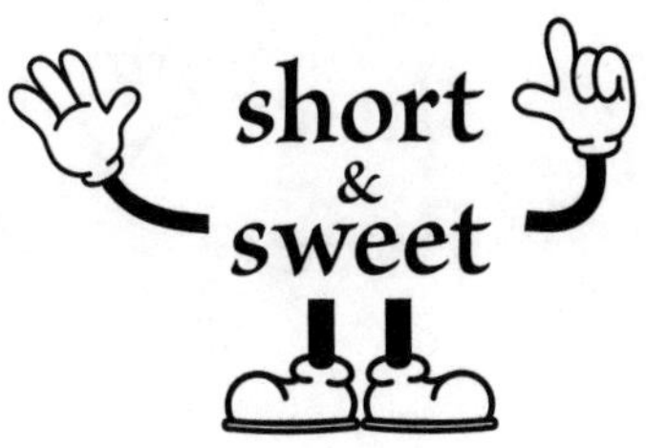

Although Rapunzel is the Disney princess with the longest hair, that doesn't mean she also has the most strands. One Disney character surpasses her: Elsa from *Frozen*.

Initially, more than 27 emotions were to be presented in the film *Inside Out*. In the end, however, only five emotions were agreed upon.

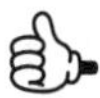

The first Disney character to sing a duet with the film's villain is Anna from *Frozen*.

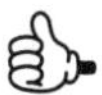

It is possible to send Disney characters a wedding invitation. In most cases, the characters will then not attend the wedding, but a response letter, small gifts, or a congratulatory certificate is often sent to the bride and groom.

Clarence Nash, best known as the voice actor for Donald Duck, also worked on *101 Dalmatians*. The barking of the dogs in the film was created by him.

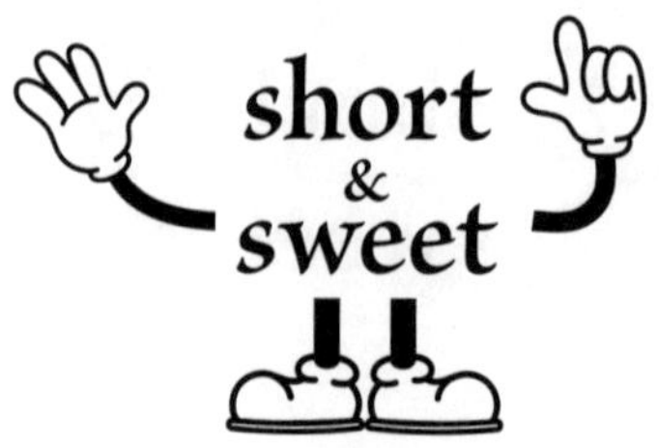

Since Walt Disney strictly refused to be called "Mr. Disney" during his lifetime, the company's employees still follow his example today and address each other casually by their first names.

Coca-Cola and Disney go hand in hand. Pepsi, on the other hand, is not sold in the Disney Parks.

Disney's motto is: "Dream, Believe, Dare, Do." With these four words, the House of Mouse has set new standards for the film industry and proven time and again that it often pays off to be brave.

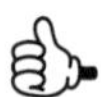

To give the character Frozone from *The Incredibles* a dubbing voice that also matched his "cool" character, director Brad Bird really wanted Samuel L. Jackson for the voice-over role.

The Idea on the Hook

As a Pixar employee, how do you convince your supervisor of a movie idea? For the idea behind *Finding Nemo*, apparently only one word was enough. Film director John Lasseter, who was responsible for the film, said he was already convinced by the idea as soon as he heard that the story was going to be about fish.

A Dragon for Mulan

For the creators of Mulan, the idea to give her a dragon as an animal companion came quite spontaneously. Since another project with a dragon was canceled, they toyed with the idea of placing the dragon somewhere else. When it became clear that Mulan should be accompanied by a dragon during her story, the question arose about what he should actually look like. The idea to create a two-headed dragon was born from the original consideration that Mulan should be accompanied by two reptiles. Later, however, it was decided to create a dragon with one head. The size of Mushu was also an essential part of the discussion. Only when the creators realized that, according to the legends, Chinese dragons can appear in many different sizes, the choice fell on the nowadays well-known small, red dragon design.

(Not) A Gig for Lotso

Known as Lotso, a pink plush bear made his first appearance in *Toy Story 3*. His first appearance? Not quite. Initially, the bear was supposed to appear in the first installment of the toy movies, and in a brief scene, he does – sort of. In *Toy Story 3,* the bear looks a bit different, but in the first part, he is already hinted at when a short camera pan during a gathering of the toys shows the shelves and the other toys which are stowed there. Among other things, a large, pink teddy bear can be also seen there. Lotso was only denied his big appearance at the time because the animators couldn't design the fur of the cuddly animal to the satisfaction of those responsible.

The Seven Sisters

Many know the feeling of having a sibling but having six of them is rather unusual. Ariel, however, should know this exact scenario. After all, she has six sisters. Together with herself, the seven daughters of Triton represent the seven seas.

A fun fact is that each name starts with an A: Ariel, Attina, Aquata, Adrina, Arista, Adella, and Alana.

The screams of children, which can be heard in *Monsters, Inc.*, are real. The animators' children helped to record them.

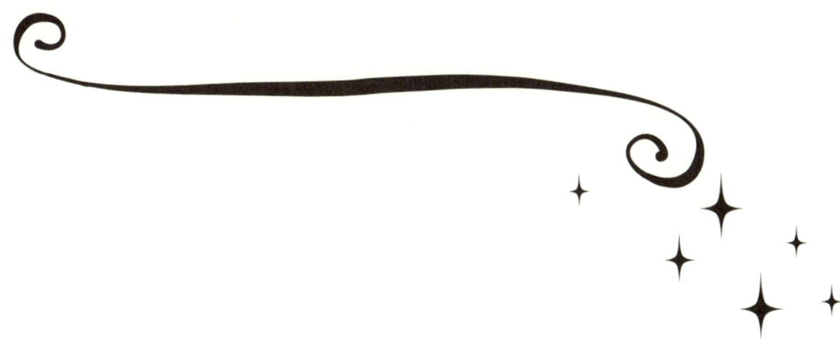

A Fox for Disney

Why was Robin Hood depicted as a fox by Disney? This decision can be traced back to the originally planned adaptation of *Renard the Fox*, also known as *Roman de Renard*. It is a medieval satirical tale set in France in the 12th and 13th centuries. The story tells of a cunning fox named Renard who tries to deceive and trick other animals. Disney had planned a film adaptation of this material, but the project was discarded. However, some ideas were adopted into other projects. Thus, Robin Hood became a fox in the Disney film of the same name.

Tarzan Swings Through the World

Like some other Disney hits, the plot of *Tarzan* is based on a book. Edgar Rice Burroughs, author of the novel *Tarzan of the Apes*, published his book as early as 1912. As the Disney production studio became increasingly famous, Burroughs firmly believed that his story would also be adapted as an animated film at some point – probably by Disney. He was proved right: In 1995, the time had finally come, and Disney started working on the film.

The Emergence of a Classic

Nowadays, *Hakuna Matata* is probably one of the most popular songs from the movie *The Lion King*. All the more surprising that the song was not initially intended to be in the script. Instead, there were plans for a song about eating bugs. The idea for the final version only came about when the research team returned from Africa. They introduced the phrase "Hakuna Matata," which the team received enthusiastically since it reminded them of *Cinderella*'s "Bibbidi-Bobbidi-Boo."

The Name Is Duck, Darkwing Duck

Darkwing Duck, the masked avenger of St. Canard, bravely fights the villains of the city. Fans will undoubtedly notice that he looks not entirely unlike a certain superhero with a black cape and a connection to bats. Instead of the black cape, however, Darkwing could also have stepped into a black tuxedo. In fact, the character was originally inspired by an entirely different movie hero. *Double O Duck*, as the working title of the series was, also clearly indicates who the role model was: James Bond. The main protagonist of the series was also different at the time. The story was supposed to revolve around Launchpad McQuack from the TV series *DuckTales*, who only appears as Darkwing's sidekick in the final version.

Disney Gets Serious

Most people probably associate Disney movies with light and funny stories for children but even the animated films sometimes take a more serious direction. With *Atlantis – The Lost Empire*, for example, the filmmakers wanted to pursue an alternative approach. The people in charge wore T-shirts with a special inscription while working to keep reminding themselves that the film should be more about explosions than songs. "Fewer songs, more explosions" was written on them.

Royalties for Artists

The 1988 release of *Cinderella* for home cinema led to a court case for Disney. The dubbing artist Ilene Woods, who had lent her voice to Cinderella in the English original as early as 1950, sued the House of Mouse after the release of *Cinderella* on video cassettes. Since no such cassettes existed at the time of the recording, they were not mentioned in her contract with Disney at the time. However, the dubbing artist wanted to be paid shares when film fans could also watch the classic at home.

Evil Snowman

Olaf, the cute snowman with the big teeth and the crooked carrot nose, was originally not supposed to appear in *Frozen*. He only came to exist because the script was rewritten. In the first drafts, he was not only placed at Elsa's side instead of Anna's, he also looked completely different. Instead of a snowman, he was planned as a penguin. In retrospect, however, the story was changed and resulted in the ever-popular snowman – fortunately!

Work from Home

At the time of the COVID-19 pandemic, almost everyone – especially at work – had to adapt to some changes. Remote work was seen as an excellent alternative to working in an office. However, the various industries and employees had to get used to it. Even Disney at times worked its wonders from home. But employees seem to have taken it with a sense of humor, as evidenced in movies like *Soul*. There, after the note "created and produced at Pixar Animation Studios," the credits added the additional note "...and in homes at least six feet away from each other throughout the Bay Area."

The Boss

As a company boss, how do you make sure that your employees use their time to work efficiently? The best way to do this is to occasionally stroll past the employees and see what's happening. Disney founder Walt Disney was also known to enjoy looking over the shoulders of the animators as they worked. Apparently, he did this so often that the employees came up with a special code to warn each other when the boss was approaching again. If someone called out, "Man in the forest," everyone would quickly get back to work. The name can be traced back to the Disney classic *Bambi* since the frightening figure there was a hunter in the forest.

Many, Many Points

Some people pay attention to every little detail when watching a movie. Here is a particularly interesting piece of information: In the film *101 Dalmatians*, there are 6,469,952 dots on the dogs' fur. So, if you want to count all of them, you should bring a lot of time. Starting with the dogs' parents, Pongo and Perdita, there is a lot to do after all. With Pongo's 72 and Perdita's 68 points, the two of them alone have an impressive 140 points to count.

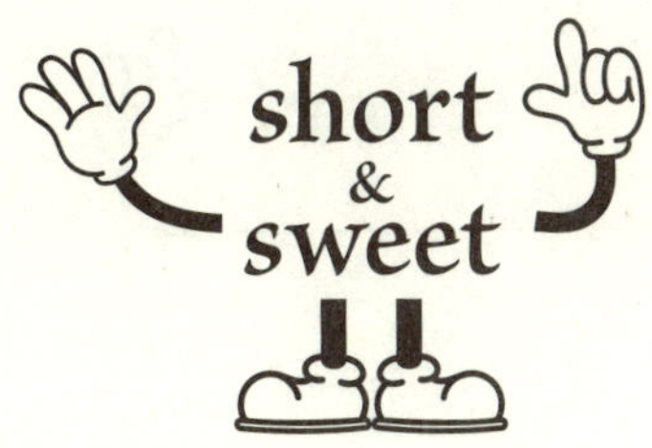

The Wise Little Hen is the first cartoon in which the Disney cult character Donald Duck appears. His first voice actor, Clarence Nash, has been nicknamed Ducky ever since.

The truck named Mater from the Pixar film *Cars* is based on a Nascar fan the filmmakers met during their research. Even the name matches: Douglas “Mater” Keever was the fan’s name.

The Disney princesses all have an official costume, which usually shows them in a ball gown. Jasmine and Raya are the only princesses dressed in pants.

A line was recorded for *Beauty and the Beast* that later did not make it into the final animated version. However, in the live-action adaptation starring Emma Watson, a question by Belle was added. After the prince’s transformation at the end of the film, she asks: “Do you think you can grow a beard?”

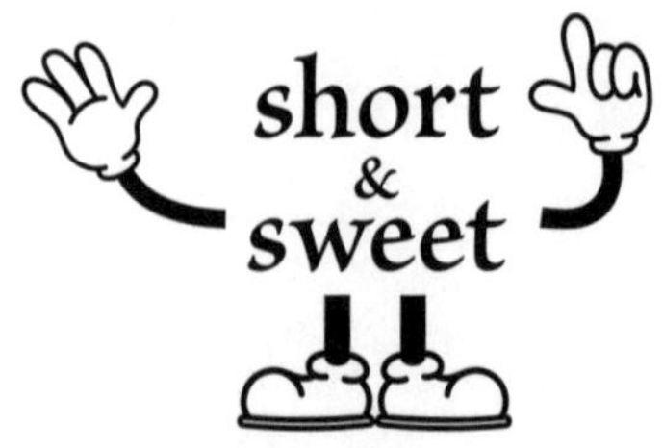

In *The Princess and the Frog*, Tiana is shown in her human form for only 19 minutes. She spends the rest of the time as a frog.

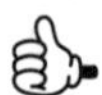

The *Star Wars* universe has officially belonged to Disney since 2012. The media giant bought the production company Lucasfilm for a whopping 4.05 billion dollars.

In order to make Aladdin's pants in the film look as natural as possible, the responsible animator Glen Keane studied several videos of the musician M. C. Hammer – known for his preference for similar pants.

Merida probably has the wildest curls among all the Disney princesses. If she straightened her hair, it would be about four feet long.

Hidden Truth

If you pay close attention while watching *Frozen*, you'll notice a few little things that are not so obvious at first. Disney always manages to include details in films that convey a hidden message. For example, the gloves in *Frozen* also have a special meaning for the events in the movie. Above all, they are associated with Elsa, who uses them to control her powers. But Hans also wears gloves, which reveals another meaning of the garments: They hide something. In Elsa's case, they suppress her true self, but Hans also hides his true nature. Accordingly, if someone wears gloves in the film, be careful: Something is being concealed here!

The First Film?

Although Disney has released many films for several decades, *The Lion King* is considered the first evening filler that actually tells a new story. After all, Disney classics like *Snow White*, *Ariel*, or *Beauty and the Beast* are all based on fairy tales or stories that existed before Disney made them real. Thus, with *The Lion King*, a new era began for the House of Mouse.

Magical World

Perhaps at first glance, the Disney film *Brave* and the *Harry Potter* series don't have much in common. However, the list of roles and actors reveals more. Four of the actors from *Harry Potter* also contributed to *Brave*. Robbie Coltrane not only plays the lovable Hagrid but also lends his voice to Lord Dingwall. Emma Thompson not only gets to introduce herself as Professor Trelawney but also as the voice of Queen Elinor. Kelly McDonald voices Merida and also stars in the role of Helena Ravenclaw in the last Potter installment, while Julie Walters, best known as Molly Weasley, took on the voice role of the witch in *Brave*. How fitting!

In Lofty Heights

How many balloons does it take to make a house fly? While thinking about this question, you might have an image of the Pixar movie *Up* in your head. In the film, the balloons let the main character's entire house fly. In purely mathematical terms, this would require over 25 million balloons, but in the movie, "only" about 20,000 balloons are used.

A Time for Every Princess

Only eight characters are considered "original" Disney princesses: Snow White, Cinderella, Aurora, Ariel, Belle, Jasmine, Mulan, and Pocahontas. It was only later that new members were added to the group. They can all be divided into three periods. The first is called the Golden Era and refers to princesses portrayed as "ideal" warm-hearted royal daughters. This era includes the group's first princesses: Snow White, Cinderella, and Aurora. The subsequent Renaissance era consists of Ariel, Belle, Jasmine, Mulan, and Pocahontas. These princesses seek adventure and are anything but quiet and obedient. The last major period, the modern era, shows princesses as independent individuals and focuses on portraying romantic relationships and love between mothers and daughters, girlfriends, or sisters. This era includes, for example, Tiana, Raya, and Merida.

Hope

Probably no other film was as crucial for the Disney corporation as *Snow White*. At the time, a whopping 1.4 million dollars were invested in the project, so the film simply had to be a success. Disney would probably have had to file for bankruptcy if it had flopped. Fortunately, however, the film did not disappoint and instead convinced all along the line. It saved Disney from financial ruin and laid the foundation for many more film successes.

Something New

For the first time, the computer animation technique CGI was used by Disney in the production of the film *Treasure Planet*. The filmmakers used the technique, which creates exact-fit images from drawn pictures or models on the computer, in combination with the traditional animation technique, especially for the artificial arm of the character Long John Silver.

Pixar Cookbook

The dishes served up in *Ratatouille* look scrumptious for a reason. The animators based their work on authentic dishes that were prepared and photographed especially for the film. Naturally, the nearly 300 dishes that were created for it were then also enjoyed by the crew.

King of Names

Lions bear the epithet "King of the Beasts"; some also call them the "King of the Jungle." This is precisely the title that the film known today as *The Lion King* was initially supposed to have. Fortunately, an employee pointed out to those responsible that lions do not actually live in the jungle.

Merry Christmas!

Somewhere there might still be some wrapping paper with a special note: the music to *You'll Be in My Heart* from the movie *Tarzan*. The idea for the song came to Phil Collins quite spontaneously at a Christmas party of his neighbors. During the party, the musician was enjoying himself at the family piano when he suddenly came up with the chords for the song. So, he immediately wrote them down on the only piece of paper he could find: a Christmas wrapping.

Scottish for the Scots

A movie set in Scotland should be spoken by people with Scottish accents, right? Wrong! At least Pixar didn't seem to think so at the beginning of *Brave*'s production. At that time, actress Reese Witherspoon was still considered as the dubbing voice for Merida. Later it was decided to give Merida a Scottish accent, wherefore the role was recast with Kelly Macdonald, since Witherspoon had an American accent.

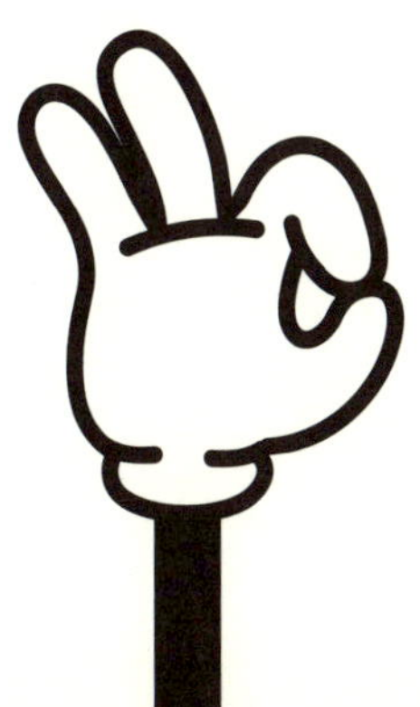

No Unnecessary Words

Dumbo, the little elephant with the big ears, is probably one of the most taciturn characters in all the Disney films. In fact, he doesn't have a single line of text in his original 1941 film, making him almost completely mute. Also, the little robot Wall-E from the movie of the same name is not a fan of big words. Apart from his name and that of his girlfriend Eve, he says remarkably little.

A Guard for Protection

After Elsa abandons her duties in *Frozen* and flees to the mountains, she is sought by her sister Anna. To protect herself and others and to keep the intruders away from her castle, Elsa creates a monster out of snow and ice during the course of the story. This monster may look a bit scary in the final film, but it was originally planned to be quite different. Since it wasn't supposed to be the first snowman that Elsa created, the monster was originally meant to resemble Olaf. In fact, it was supposed to be a sort of giant version of the popular snowman. However, the filmmakers decided that a more significant Olaf might not be intimidating enough and decided to change the monster's design.

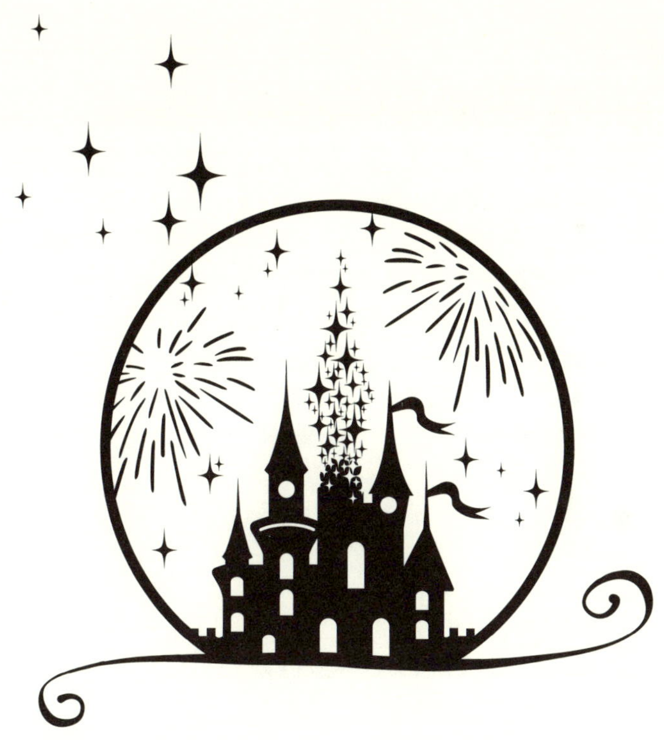

Ariel is the only Disney princess to become a mother and even have a daughter in her films.

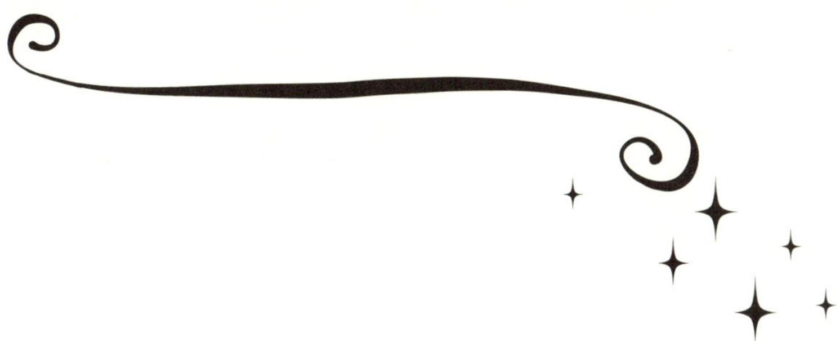

A Real Boy!

It's hard to make a wooden boy look cute. At least the artists behind *Pinocchio* needed a few attempts before Disney founder Walt Disney liked the design concept. The biggest difficulty was combining cuteness and the doll structure. The solution eventually came through Milt Kahl, who suggested to first focus on drawing a cutely rendered boy. The screws and artificial arms were then added afterward.

Last-Minute Change

VHS video cassettes often have trailers of upcoming movie titles before the main film. The 1996 VHS version of *Toy Story* also includes such previews. One of these trailers is for the movie *Hercules*. Among others, the preview shows an excerpt from the film, which did not appear in the final version. In the scene where Hercules meets Meg for the first time and saves her from Nessus, Phil gives him a little advice after the rescue. He should not neglect his defense because of a pair of big blue eyes. In the final film, however, it can be seen that Meg does not have blue eyes but purple ones. Initially, this was planned differently, as Phil's remark proves. In the published version, the line was then changed. Here Hercules should not be distracted by a pair of goo-goo eyes.

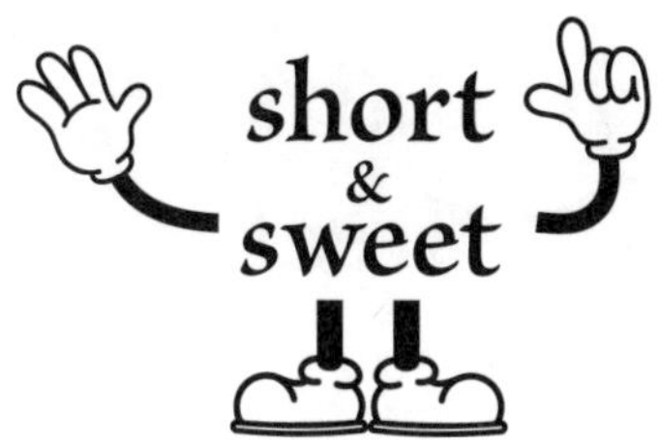

If the character Eve from *Wall-E* reminds some viewers of the design of Apple's iPhone and iPod products, there is a very specific reason for this. The designer of both products, Jonathan Ive, was also involved in the design of the film character.

Before *Beauty and the Beast*, the villains in Disney princess movies were exclusively women. Only Gaston put an end to this rule.

Inside the Cinderella Castle of Disney World, in addition to a restaurant, there is also the Bibbidi-Bobbiddi boutique.

On special occasions, time capsules are sometimes buried and then recovered years later. The Disneyland Resort in California also houses such a capsule. It was buried in front of the big castle in 1995 and will not be dug up again until July 17, 2035.

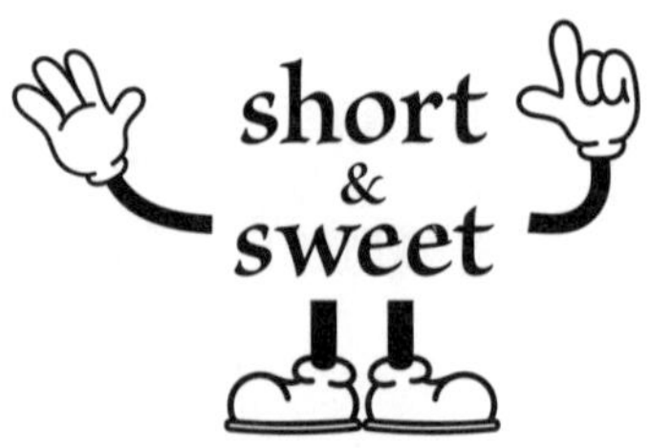

The construction of the Ice Palace in *Frozen* presented the animators with unprecedented challenges. A whole 50 people were involved in the process.

Known today as Disney's Hollywood Studios, the theme park was originally intended as an actual production studio. Operating at the time under the name Disney-MGM Studios, some films were even made there before the site was converted into a theme park.

Buzz Lightyear was initially supposed to be given a different name: Lunar Larry.

Donald Duck's nephews – Huey, Dewey, and Louie – are well-known to Disney fans. Lesser known is the fact that Donald even has a son of his own. The little duckling is only shown in the short *How to Have an Accident at Work* and was never heard of again.

The Real Kingdom

Viewers of animated films usually assume that everything they see is the product of the creators' imagination. Sometimes, however, the animators are inspired by real-life events or places. This is also the case in the Disney animated hit *Tangled*. Although the film is loosely based on the Brothers Grimm fairy tale, the environment shown, such as the construction of the kingdom or even the surroundings of the valley in which Rapunzel's tower is located, are also based on real places. For example, the French municipality of Rocamadour served as the model for the hidden valley and the French rocky island of Mont-Saint-Michel for the royal city.

Behind the Stars

Amateur astronomers might notice a small detail they disagree with while watching *Hercules*. When Hades gets his future prophesied, six planets line up. Connoisseurs of the starry sky naturally know that there are more than six planets in our solar system. However, at the time of Ancient Greece, in which *Hercules* is set, only six of them were known.

Important Scene

One of the most famous scenes from *Sleeping Beauty* is the *Once Upon a Dream* singing sequence. During production, however, this scene, in which Aurora and Prince Phillip meet for the first time, caused some trouble. The editing of this sequence even almost blew the entire film budget. The reason: Walt Disney. The company's founder was just too hard to please and kept demanding that the scene be reworked because he didn't like one or two details in it.

Donald on the Field

The University of Oregon sports team has a mascot like no other. The Oregon Ducks didn't just choose any duck as their mascot, but the drake par excellence: Donald Duck. A license agreement with Disney made it possible. In 1984, Donald even graduated from the university. More than 3,000 fans gathered at the airport especially for the event. Donald, who came to visit, was officially presented with his honorary graduate robe and accompanying hat. The famous duck also received a congratulatory letter signed by numerous residents of the area.

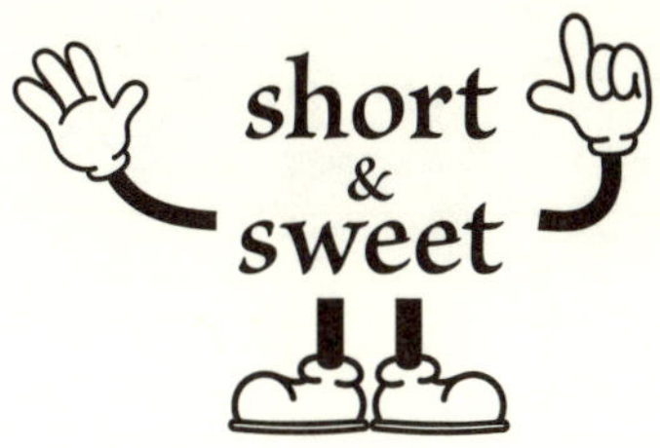

Most Pixar films feature talking animals or humanized objects. The studio's first film to feature an all-human cast was *The Incredibles*.

Only two of the official Disney princesses have siblings: Ariel and Merida.

The fact that many Disney characters grow up without a mother could be due to the circumstance that Walt Disney also lost his mother very early.

Disney World Resort in Florida is almost as big as the city of San Francisco.

All of the basketball players who play on the Wildcats team in *High School Musical* had to participate in an audition. Even if it wasn't for a speaking role, they had to prove their skills in advance.

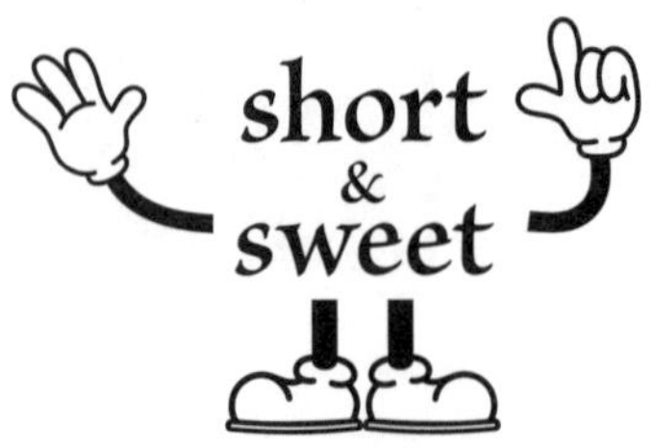

Snow White was the first female fictional character to be honored with a star on the Hollywood Walk of Fame.

Viewers might notice that trains often appear in Disney movies. This is most likely due to the fact that Walt Disney was a big train fan. There was even the Carolwood Pacific Railroad in his garden – a miniature train track complete with a tunnel.

The last Disney princess Walt Disney himself could witness on the big screen was Aurora from *Sleeping Beauty.*

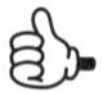

The life expectancy of the people in *Wall-E* seems to have increased considerably. From the images of the spaceship captains, it appears they held an average tenure of 135 years.

Pixelated Figures

Since various characters from different franchises appear in the movie *Wreck-It Ralph*, the filmmakers initially toyed with the idea of keeping these characters in their original drawing and animation styles. However, since that would also mean showing Ralph as a pixelated 8-bit character for the entire film, they ultimately decided against this proposal. After all, it would make the film's main character seem less approachable.

Ideas From Far Away

When it comes to a new film project, the makers first have to gather ideas. Once the rough concept is in place, fine-tuning comes into play. For the filmmakers, this involves one thing above all: research. Even when it comes to finding names, those responsible are often inspired by the location of the action. For example, the terms of some Disney characters refer directly to their location and the local language. For Simba from *The Lion King*, a name was chosen that means lion in Swahili. Baloo, the bear from *The Jungle Book*, is derived from the word bhalu – Hindi for bear.

Loyalty Pays Off

Walt Disney, the founder of the media giant company, seemed to have a lot of affection for his housekeeper Thelma Howard. For Christmas and her birthday, her employer gave her Disney company stock as a gift. By the time of her death, she held nine million dollars' worth of Disney stock. The Disney founder stated that Thelma was practically family, so the generous gift is unsurprising.

Barbie, the Superstar

Among other things, *Toy Story* also features a number of toys and characters that are familiar to children around the world. Barbie is one of them. In the first part of the popular series, Barbie was even supposed to have played a more important role. Initially, it was planned to suggest a possible love story between her and Woody, and Barbie was also supposed to have a more significant influence on the main plot. For example, towards the end of the film, she was to be celebrated as the savior of the group of friends around Woody, Buzz, and co. Yet, the owner of the Barbie rights, Mattel, rejected the proposal. At the time, they didn't believe the film would succeed and were afraid Barbie could lose popularity. Ultimately, however, the film exceeded all expectations and became an animated hit. After this success, Mattel also gave its approval so that Barbie was allowed to shine in the sequels of the film with more significant appearances.

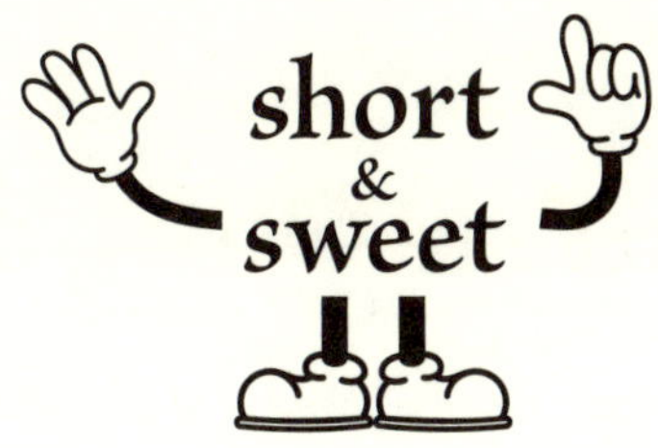

During a ride on Buzz Lightyear's Space Ranger Spin, daring adventurers can earn points. However, one can only advance to the Galactic Hero rank with a score of 999,999. If you hit this score, you can get a free sticker at a souvenir shop.

It can get pretty hot at Disney's Hollywood Studios. But a quick cool down isn't far away: Just take a trip to the giant umbrella built at the Streets of America area. There, a switch in the floor makes it easy to activate the umbrella and causes a short downpour.

Eleanor Audley apparently had a particularly evil-sounding voice. At least, if you judge her by the fact that the US voice actress voiced both Maleficent in *Sleeping Beauty* and Cinderella's evil stepmother.

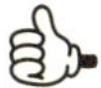

Lady from *Lady and the Tramp* is modeled after a real dog whose name was also Lady.

Real French

Although *The Hunchback of Notre Dame* is set in France, this doesn't mean the project was produced there. However, French Disney employees are indeed responsible for some details of the architecture and landscape shown in the film. For the film, some of these tasks were given specifically to the Disney studio in Paris so the film would be as authentic as possible. About 100 French animators worked on the project.

How Time Flies...

It usually takes several years before an idea is actually turned into a film. Walt Disney already had the first idea for the film *The Little Mermaid* back in the 1930s. Nevertheless, it took several decades before the film was released in cinemas. The Disney founder probably had a very different idea for the movie at the time because the technology had advanced so far that the makers could even use computer animation technology in a few scenes. Something Walt Disney would not have imagined.

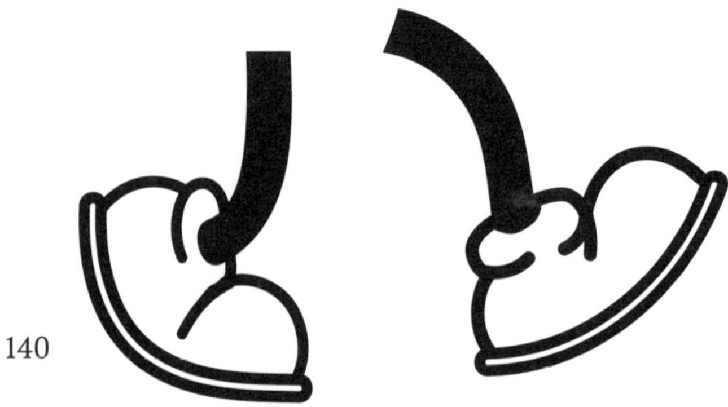

No Disney Food

Disney Springs is a park in Orlando, Florida, where guests can experience all sorts of events. Unlike other Disney Parks, visitors can't expect colossal roller coasters or a Cinderella castle here, but various other attractions. In addition to shopping and smaller amusement devices such as a carousel, a bowling alley, a movie theater, or several places to go for music-loving guests, even Cirque du Soleil performs here. Of course, the right food should also be on offer. Numerous restaurants provide catering in the park. However, not all of these restaurants do belong to Disney itself. About 13 of the establishments are not part of the media giant.

"Old" Technology

Although the film *Wall-E* was mainly created on computer, the intention was to give the impression that the film was shot with a real camera. Director Andrew Stanton, therefore, wanted to include minor "camera errors," such as reflections or a blurred focus setting. A consultant was also hired to show the animators exactly how the scene would have been shot with a real camera.

Confusing Relationship

Strictly speaking, the Disney characters Ariel and Hercules should be related. Hercules is known to be the son of Zeus. He, in turn, has a brother named Poseidon. According to the story, Poseidon's son is Triton, Ariel's father. Thus, Ariel would be the daughter of Hercules' cousin – meaning that she is Hercules' second cousin.

Princess in Blue

Princesses have always been considered stereotypes. Most people probably imagine them as blond with a pink dress. Disney, however, broke with this notion from a very early stage. Snow White, Belle, Elsa – they all couldn't be more different. But they have one thing in common: They wear blue. Over the years, Disney has repeatedly proven that princesses can also be very individual. Thus, prejudices are regularly challenged. Fans like to interpret the fact that some of Disney's royal representatives are often seen in blue clothing as the company wanting to express that blue doesn't just have to be considered a color for men. Besides, not all princesses have to wear pink all the time.

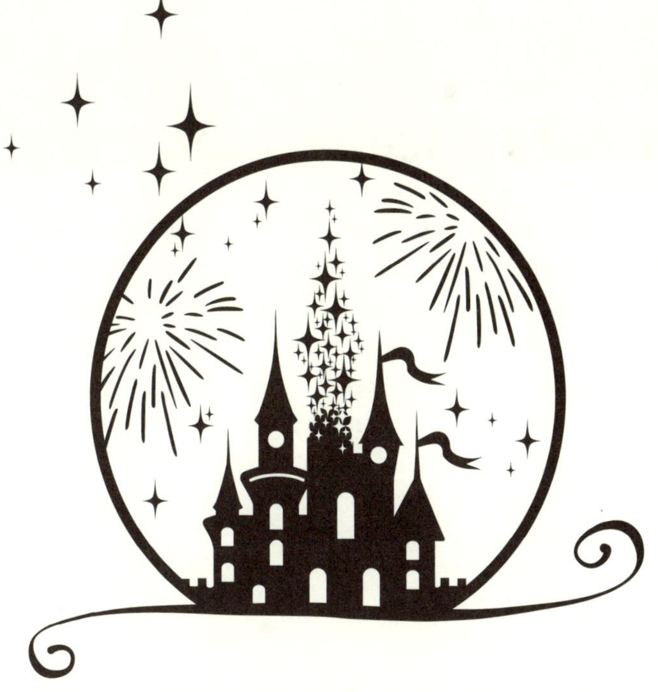

When Walt Disney won an Honorary Oscar for *Snow White and the Seven Dwarfs*, the trophy was a very special one. The statue consisted of the known golden figure and seven little ones, picturing the seven dwarfs.

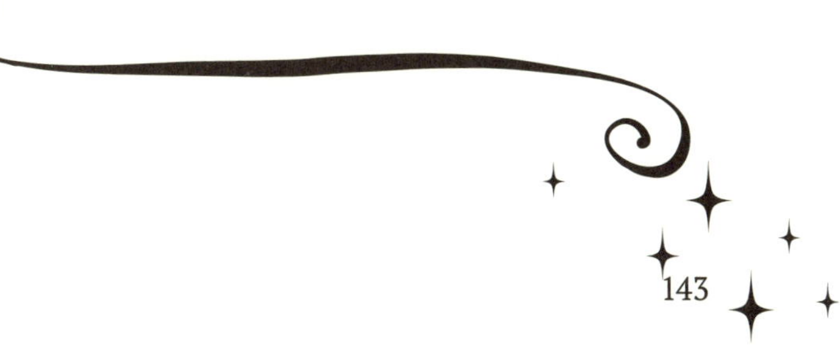

Cold As Ice

One of *Frozen's* most famous scenes is probably where Elsa creates her own ice castle. The castle is created only by her magic and has a few magical properties. For example, it changes color depending on Elsa's mood at that moment. The castle seems to glow reddish if she is very agitated, scared, or angry. If she is sad, on the other hand, a purple glow appears on the ice. Even though Elsa always tries not to show her feelings to the outside world – her castle clearly reflects them.

Magical Change

Mickey Mouse has been very convincing in many roles since his first appearance. Particularly popular is his portrayal of the sorcerer's apprentice in the Disney film *Fantasia.* However, this role was almost assigned to someone other than Mickey. Dopey from *Snow White and the Seven Dwarfs* was also up for it. The fairy tale adaptation was so popular that those responsible thought it would be smart to bring the little dwarf back to the big screen. Yet, Walt Disney, had Mickey in mind from the beginning of the project and was not dissuaded from this decision. He was convinced with the idea that everyone could identify with Mickey, which probably wouldn't have been the case with Dopey.

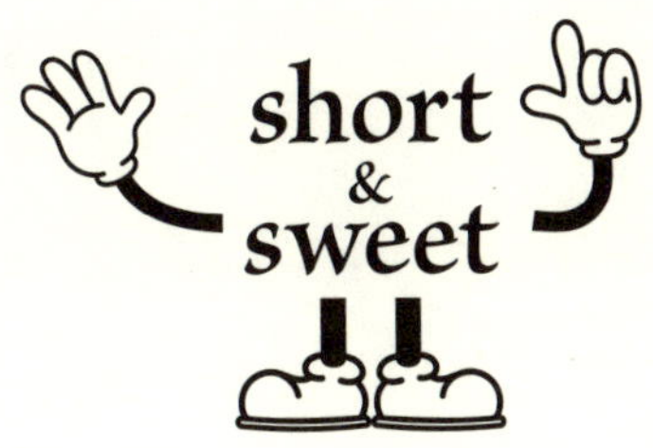

Steve Jobs made his first billion, mainly thanks to Pixar. Since he owned most of the shares in the animation company, he managed to get the company listed on the stock exchange. It was a complete success for him: The share price shot up.

The Cinderella Castle in the Magic Kingdom consists of 18 towers. 13 gargoyles have also made themselves comfortable at the castle.

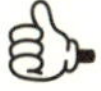

Donald Duck has a middle name: Fauntleroy.

In *Snow White and the Seven Dwarfs*, a few songs can be heard, but there could have been many more. A whole 25 songs were composed especially for the film, but in the end, only eight made it into the final version.

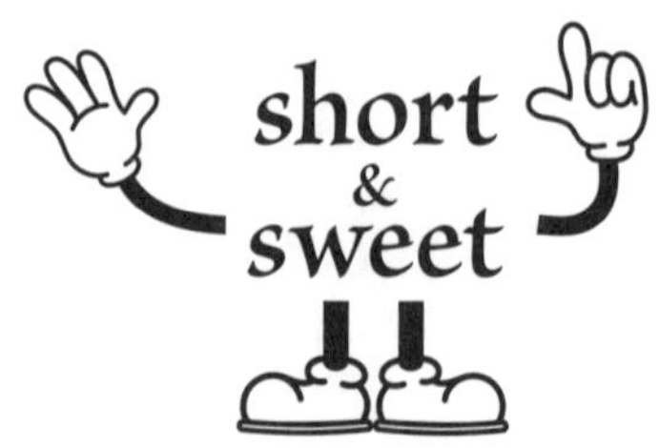

Stitch's voice in *Lilo & Stitch* is spoken by the film's director. Chris Sanders was only supposed to step in for the test animations. In the end, however, the filmmakers liked the voice so much that they decided not to cast a new voice actor for the role.

The former Axiom spaceship captains shown in the film *Wall-E* are all based on Pixar employees. The images show the studio's creators as caricatures.

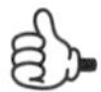

The dog that barks at Remy when he first emerges from the Paris sewers in *Ratatouille* looks suspiciously like Dug from *Up*.

In the early days of the Disney studios, female animators were not hired. Walt Disney believed that women were not creative enough for the job. Nowadays of course, things are different, and women are also part of the animation team.

Born for the Role

Normally, a film role exists first and then a suitable actor (or a voice actor in the case of animated films) must be found for it. In retrospect, viewers usually can't imagine the respective voice actor in any other way. With *Aladdin*, however, this principle was reversed. It was clear early on that Robin Williams should speak the Genie. The character was therefore written especially for him.

No Reason to Panic

Near the Haunted Mansion in Disney World, there's a lot to discover. After all, it's not just in the movies that Disney pays attention to every little detail; the theme parks and their design also benefit from the meticulous attention of those responsible. For example, the lawn next to the Haunted Mansion features a pet cemetery. Upon closer inspection, however, it quickly becomes clear that there is no reason to be afraid here. The tombstones all contain inscriptions, but these are intended to make the guests laugh – names like I. M. Ready, Manny Festation, or Rustin Peese are fun to say even after the actual attraction.

Conflicts in the Animal Kingdom

Lions against hyenas, or rather lions against baboons? This was probably a question the makers of the Disney hit *The Lion King* had to ask themselves. In initial considerations, the film was not supposed to accompany a conflict between hyenas and lions, as is known today, but rather revolve around a dispute between lions and baboons. Scar would not have appeared as a "bad uncle" but would have been the leader of the apes. Then again, Rafiki, a wise if unusual monkey in the final film, was supposed to slip into the role of a cheetah. Nowadays, it's hard to imagine what the film would have looked like if these ideas had been adopted.

The Real Warrior

The film *Mulan* tells the story of a young woman who – disguised as a man – joins the imperial troops to defend China. The model for the successful movie from Disney is a Chinese legend. Some changes were made for the film adaptation, but the basic idea remained the same. By the way, it is unclear whether Mulan really existed. Her story has been retold over time, but there is no concrete evidence that it is true.

The Prince Without a Name

For decades, girls worldwide have been dreaming of this moment: feeling like Cinderella for once and meeting the Prince Charming of their dreams. But what is actually his name? Generally speaking, the prince from the Disney film *Cinderella* is known as Prince Charming. But if you watch the movie again and pay close attention, you'll see that his name is never actually mentioned.

Color Variety

All princesses are blonde and wear pink dresses. Not so at Disney! In fact, only one Disney princess is really blonde: Aurora from *Sleeping Beauty*. Some fans are sure to perk up at this statement. After all, aren't Cinderella, Rapunzel, and Elsa also blonde? No. Cinderella is considered a strawberry blonde with a soft red tint in her hair. Elsa, on the other hand, is platinum blonde. Rapunzel, strictly speaking, is a brunette. Only the magic in her hair makes it appear blonde.

"Short" Names

The little robot Wall-E from the movie of the same name apparently has a very special name. On the one hand, there is a rumor that the name is based on Walt Elias Disney, the founder of the House of Mouse. On the other hand, it is said to be an acronym. Hence, Wall-E stands for "Waste Allocation Load Lifter Earth-Class." Such a description also exists for Eve. The abbreviation stands for "Extra-terrestrial Vegetation Evaluator."

True Rogues

Over time, there have always been crime gangs that have made it to national or even international prominence. One such group was the Barker-Karpis gang, which was up to mischief in the early 20th century. The gang, which consisted mainly of members of one family, was even the inspiration for some Duckburg chapters years later. The Beagle Boys, who keep running into Scrooge and his nephews, are based on that very family. One unmistakable reference: The head of the Beagle Boys is called Ma Beagle and even outwardly refers slightly to "Ma" Barker, known as the criminal gang's matriarch.

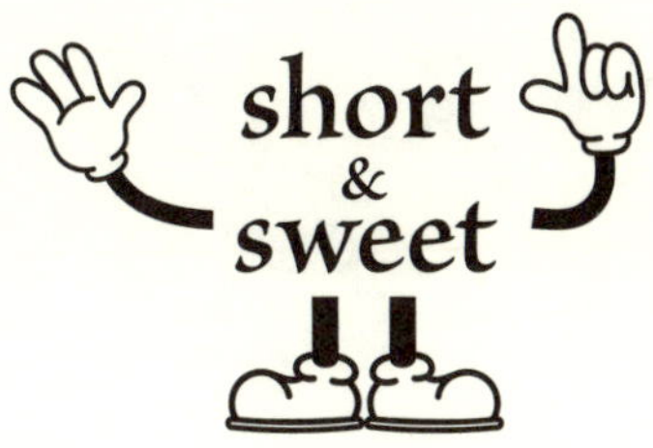

Toy Story became the first animated film ever to be nominated at the Oscars in the "Best Original Screenplay" category.

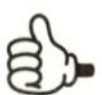

Many people think the little fairy Tinkerbell from *Peter Pan* was modeled on Marilyn Monroe. However, this is not entirely true. In fact, the actress Margaret Kelly was used as a model.

On a single day, about 50,000 visitors enter the Disney World grounds.

To ensure that the characters in *The Incredibles* really look like individual figures, the animators based their work on real faces. Since the smiles and teeth were especially important, the staff had themselves photographed so that they could use the images as a reference.

Fittingly, the name Tiana comes from the Greek word for princess.

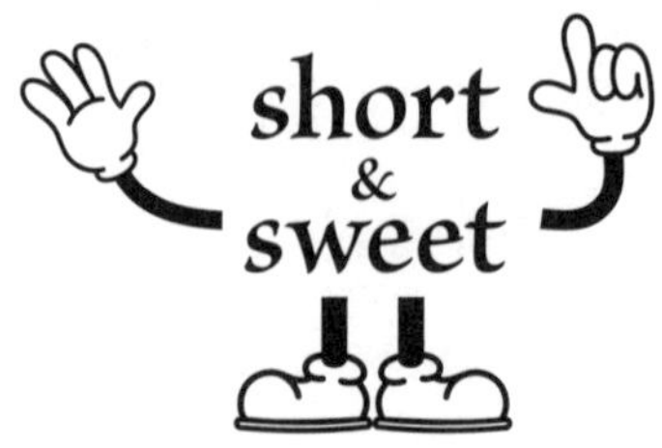

Strictly speaking, the popular Doritos chips are a Disney invention – or at least a Disneyland invention. A restaurant called Casa de Fritos came up with the idea of repurposing dry tortillas in 1966. Later, Frito-Lay bought the rights to the recipe and made the snack famous worldwide.

In the original plan, the story of *Cinderella* was to be told by talking animals.

The names of the three gargoyles from *The Hunchback of Notre Dame* have a specific meaning. While Laverne was named after the director's wife, the other two gargoyles were named after the author of the original novel, Victor Hugo.

The initial designs for Aurora's bourgeois appearance in *Sleeping Beauty* were inspired by cinema icon Audrey Hepburn and her early films.

A Very Famous Race Car

Lightning McQueen from *Cars* holds quite a few secrets. No less than two Pixar employees have a connection to the car, and another animated film is also associated with the racing car in some way. The number emblazoned on the car is number 95 in the finished film, but it was initially supposed to be number 57. The number was considered to refer to 1957, the birth year of John Lasseter, who is responsible for numerous Pixar hits like *Toy Story* or *Finding Nemo.* Ultimately, however, the number was changed to 95, a reference to the year *Toy Story* was released. The name Lightning McQueen is a tribute to the supervising animator Glenn McQueen. The name part "McQueen" was retained in all international film versions. On the other hand, the first name "Lightning" was changed in some variants, which is why in written mentions usually only "McQueen" was used. This way, the animators did not have to adapt the script for each individual version.

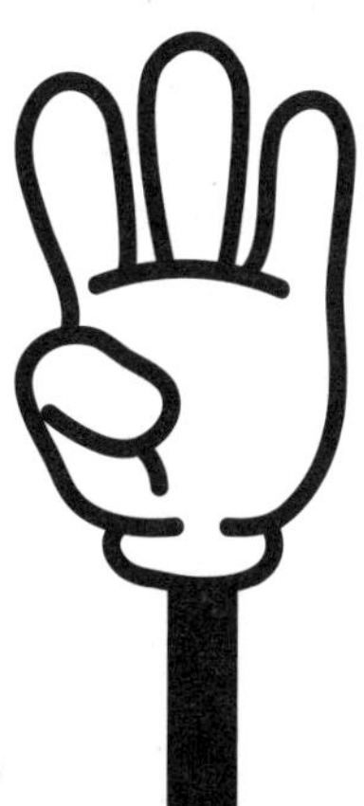

Curious Finds

It seems nearly impossible to avoid losing something during a visit to the Disney Parks. In Disneyland's Magic Kingdom alone, over 200 pairs of abandoned sunglasses are collected every day. Therefore, sunglasses are far from unusual for the employees at the Lost & Found stations. But when it comes to prosthetic legs or glass eyes, even the most hardened employees are likely to go wide-eyed. The examples are not fictitious: Such finds have actually been handed in at the counters.

Talking Machines

Often characters with a limited vocabulary are also given a voice. For example, this applies to the robot Wall-E from the movie of the same name and R2-D2 from *Star Wars*. However, the two are connected not only because they are both robots but also because their voices were developed by the same sound designer. Ben Burtt had already convinced audiences with his work on *E.T. The Extra-Terrestrial* and *Star Trek*, so he was the perfect choice for this. For *Wall-E* alone, he recorded around 2,500 sounds, many of them created in a junkyard.

The Mixture Makes the Difference

For several years now, most animated Disney films have been produced using 3D optics. However, in some movies, you can still find some components that revert to the 2D variant. A well-known example of this is the film *Moana*. Here, the viewer might think that the images were created almost exclusively with 3D animation, but in fact, the 2D look is hidden in small details. For example, Maui's tattoos were drawn by hand in two dimensions. After *Winnie the Pooh*, which was released in 2011, *Moana* is the first film to combine the two techniques.

Final Decision

After *Let It Go*, the song *Do You Want to Build a Snowman* is probably one of the most popular songs from *Frozen*. Yet, it almost didn't make it into the final film. Although the song was already recorded, it was later cut out of the film. It was only in the final stages of production that the decision was made to include the song again. In retrospect, that was probably a good decision, considering how popular the song is with fans.

A New Project

It was fortunate that entrepreneurs and companies like M.T. Lott Co. bought a few acres of land in Florida – otherwise, there would be no Disney World today. But shouldn't Walt Disney have been the buyer of the land? Correct, and he was. However, the media mogul used cover companies for the new project. Disney, under several different names and companies, purchased what was ultimately over 12,000 hectares. His name only became known when he bought a large part of the land. He probably wanted to conceal his plans for the time being to avoid possible competition from other buyers.

A Real Princess

Strictly speaking, Pocahontas is not a princess but a chief's daughter. But she is still one of the official Disney princesses. Another special feature: Pocahontas is the only one among the Disney princesses who is based on an actual historical figure. Also in history, Pocahontas belonged to the indigenous people from North America and was confronted with colonization. Besides Pocahontas, also Mulan could be based on a historical figure. However, since her story is a Chinese legend, it is unclear whether the character really existed.

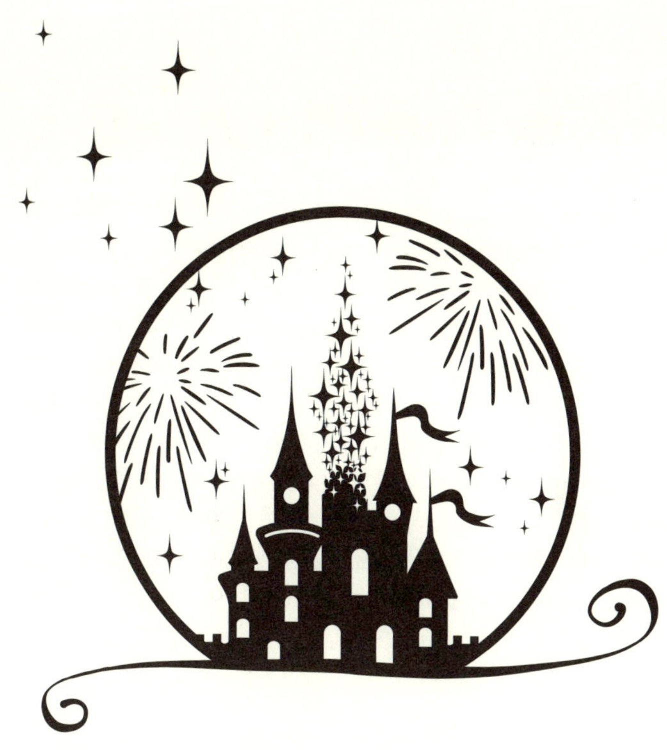

Goofy was not always called by that name. Initially, his name was Dippy Dawg.

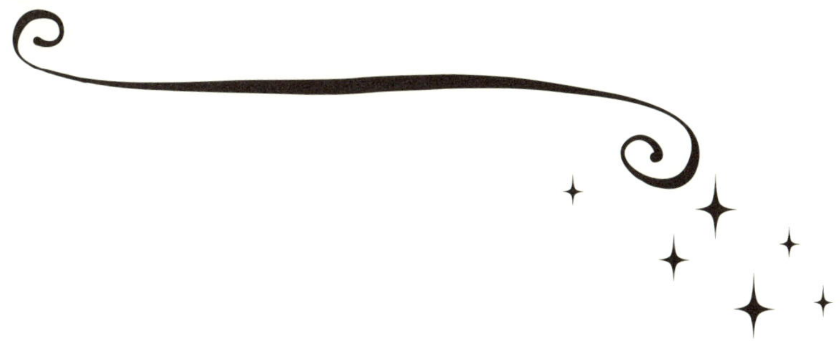

Family Sticks Together

Family is essential for the Madrigals from Disney's *Encanto*. Of course, this is easy to tell from the story, but it also becomes quite clear when paying attention to the small details that the Disney animators have incorporated into the film. For example, if you take a closer look at Mirabel's father, you can tell right away how much he loves his daughters. His clothes speak for themselves: In addition to a sock with dumbbells on it, which Luisa would like, he also wears a sock with Mirabel's typical embroidery. Moreover, there is a purple flower on his vest that points to Isabela.

Frozen Founder

Many Disney fans are still convinced that the founder of the corporation, Walt Disney, had himself frozen to be revived in the future. The rumor arose when a journalist claimed to have seen Walt Disney in a frozen cylinder in hospital. The theory is supported by the fact that the founder does not have a real grave. Instead, he is said to be cremated. The only place for fans to commemorate him is a memorial plaque at Forest Garden. The rumors have persisted for years, although an official statement from Disney's daughter confirmed that this was just a crazy fan theory.

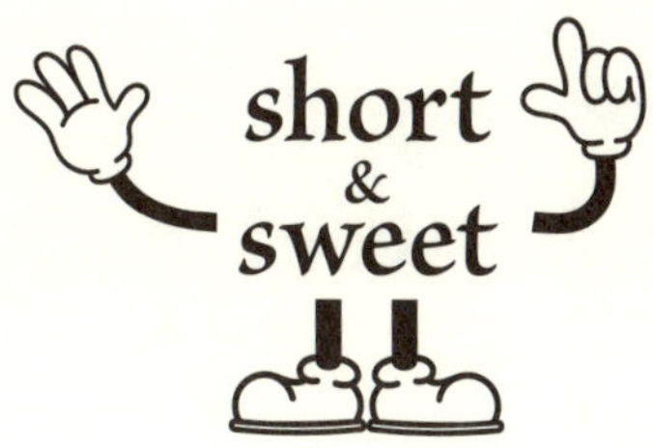

Fittingly for the story of two sisters, *Frozen* was the first Disney animated film directed by a woman.

A very unique voice is used several times in the announcements at the Disney Parks. Known from *The Grinch* animated film or as the voice of Tony the Tiger, Thurl Ravenscroft can also be heard at attractions such as the Haunted Mansion, the Mark Twain River Boat, or It's A Small World.

Every now and then, the animators of a film allow themselves a little fun. For example, they create characters based on their colleagues. This is what happened in Dumbo. Two clowns are modeled after employees Art Babbitt and Jack Kinney.

The actress who voices Eve in *Wall-E* was never hired for the job. In fact, Elissa Knight was a Pixar employee who was only supposed to fill in as a placeholder for rehearsal. Later, however, she took over the voice-over role completely.

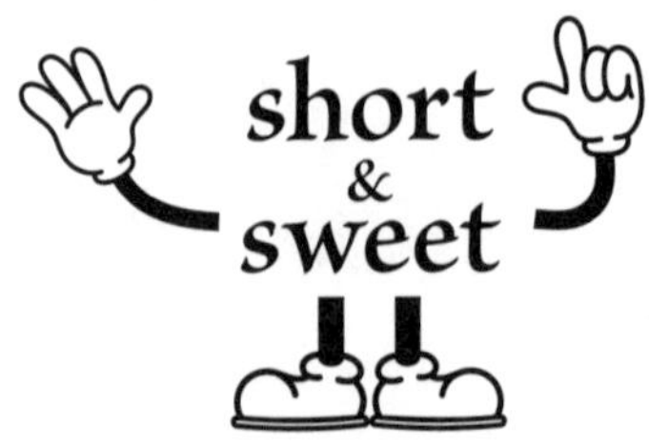

Apparently, tourists in Paris do prefer other places over the Louvre or the Eiffel Tower. The city's most popular destination is Disneyland – even though the park is about a 45-minute drive from the metropolis.

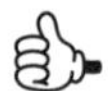

Walt Disney knew from a very early stage that he would someday make his own film out of the fairy tale Snow White. He got the idea for *Snow White and the Seven Dwarfs* at the age of 15 after seeing a silent film based on the story.

If you compare the two foxes from *Zootopia* and *Robin Hood*, something stands out: The two seem to have the same clothing style. Is that a coincidence? Probably not.

An often-repeated feature in Pixar films is the appearance of a delivery truck from Pizza Planet. In *The Incredibles*, however, fans look in vain for this Easter Egg.

Greetings from Reality

For the first time in the history of the Pixar production studio, *Wall-E* mixed animation and live-action content. There are a few scenes with real actors in the final film. Probably the most obvious is the one where Wall-E watches the 1969 film *Hello, Dolly!* The scenes were integrated into the animated movie without any changes.

The Right Technique

You go on a safari wanting to see lions, elephants, and zebras; but then, no animal is in sight. To ensure this doesn't happen, the people in charge of Kilimanjaro Safaris at Disney World's Zoo have devised a few tricks to lure the animals or bring them to highly visible locations. For example, the lion does not lie majestically on the big rock by pure chance, where visitors can have an excellent view of it. The place on the rock is equipped with air conditioning and is especially popular with animals. The gorillas only show themselves from such a short distance because there they are rewarded with raisins, and the elephants even come very close to the safari vehicles. No wonder – on the roofs of the vehicles they always find honey (quite by accident, of course).

The Price of Success

The completion of the film *Cars* led to a veritable revolution. The film was so realistic that it quickly became the new benchmark for all subsequent animated films. Of course, this reputation came at a price: The film's creators had to invest an insane amount of time in its production. This was the first Pixar film to use the so-called ray-tracing technology, which ensures that light incidence and reflections in the animation can be calculated and shown by a computer. However, the revolutionary technology also meant that it took about 17 hours to create a single image – about 1/24 of a second.

Royal Names

There could be much more to the names of Lilo and her sister Nani than is immediately apparent. The story of the two in *Lilo & Stitch* takes place in Hawaii, which is the first clue to a possible deeper meaning of the names. After all, the last reigning queen of Hawaii was named Liliuokalani. Both Lilo and Nani are part of this name to some extent. Another clue, which probably can't be just coincidence, is Nani's song to say goodbye to Lilo. The song *Aloha 'Oe* was originally written by Liliuokalani herself. Therefore, the connection to the Hawaiian queen exists on several levels.

Last Second Change

Pocahontas is one of the Disney princess films in which animals cannot speak. Originally, however, this was planned differently. Instead of Meeko, the raccoon, Pocahontas was to be accompanied by a turkey named Redfeather in the initial plans for the film. The bird had even been already assigned a dubbing voice: John Candy, comedian and actor, was to lend him his voice. Later, however, the filmmakers decided not to include any talking animals in the film. Thus, John Candy and the turkey were no longer part of the plan.

Overarching Economy

The creative minds behind Pixar films always create subtle connections between the studio's various films. For example, the logo of the Buy-N-Large company, or BNL for short, can be spotted in several films. The fictional company first became known through the movie *Wall-E,* but it is also essential for Buzz Lightyear from *Toy Story.* The company apparently manufactures the batteries for Buzz.

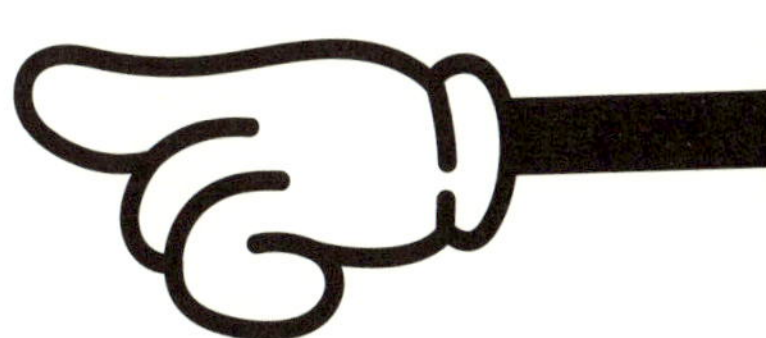

Apple Car

In honor of Apple co-founder Steve Jobs, Disney had a white race car with the Apple logo and the number 84 (the year the first Apple Macintosh computer was released) drive around the track in the movie *Cars*. Steve Jobs received this special tribute because he was one of Disney's largest shareholders and even sat on the company's board of directors.

The Misfortune of the Curious

Who would have thought that *Raiders of the Lost Ark* owed one of its most iconic scenes to the adventures of Scrooge McDuck? Nowadays, almost everyone associates the giant boulder chasing *Indiana Jones* with that very franchise. However, the idea might have come directly from a 1954 comic about Scrooge McDuck called *The Seven Cities of Cibola*. After all, *Indiana Jones* creator George Lucas is a big fan of the series. In the comic, Scrooge and his three grandsons find a treasure in a forgotten city. Yet, removing this treasure triggers a trap – a boulder. This certainly sounds familiar to many movie lovers...

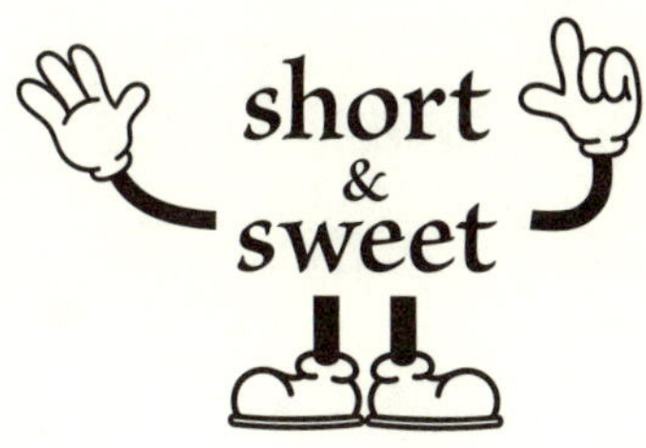

Some places in Disneyland can only be accessed with the help of a secret password. This is the case with the Riverboat Ride at Disneyland. If you ask an employee to visit the captain's cabin of the Mark Twain riverboat, you may be allowed to signal to other boats and even steer the ship yourself.

Billy Crystal could have lent his voice not only to the green spherical monster Mike Wazowski from *Monsters, Inc.* He was also offered the voice role of Buzz Lightyear in *Toy Story.* According to his own statement, he regrets in retrospect that he turned down this role at the time.

In *The Princess and the Frog,* Tiana and Prince Naveen try to have Mama Odie lift the spell that has turned them into frogs. The design of the elderly lady was inspired by several different characters. In the end, Odie was based on a mixture of Yoda, author Coleen Salley, and comedian Moms Mabley.

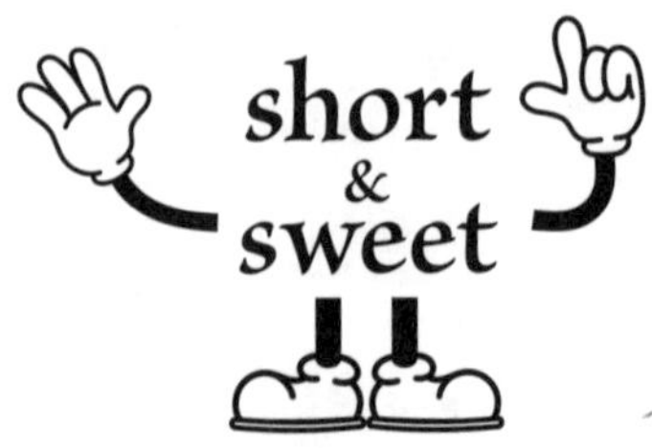

Mickey Mouse's companion is best known by the name Minnie. Yet, her full name is Minerva Mouse.

Except for Tiana from *The Princess and the Frog*, no other Disney princess has dimples when she smiles.

During the Second World War, a gas mask was created in the shape of Mickey Mouse. Children were supposed to be less afraid of gas attacks with it.

To ensure that the animals in the Disney films could be animated as realistically as possible, real animals were often brought to the production set to study their movements. Before the release of *Bambi*, for example, one could have met two deer in the studio.

The most purchased souvenirs at Disney Parks are Mickey Mouse ears.

Back on the Screen

Mickey and the Beanstalk was not supposed to be just a short film but a complete evening filler. Due to the Second World War, however, the production was affected, and it was decided to bring Mickey at least as part of the film *Fun and Fancy Free* on the screen in 1947. It was the last motion picture where Walt Disney lent his voice to the mouse.

Rodents at Home

Rats have always been considered vermin. Especially near food, no one wants to see them. Unless, of course, the rat is the celebrity chef Remy from the animated film *Ratatouille*. The little rat is extremely popular not only with restaurant patrons in the film but also with movie lovers. When the film was released in 2007, it created a real hype about pet rats. The rodents, it turns out, are not only very clean but also brilliant animals if you take care of them properly. According to a pet shop in Great Britain, requests for rats increased by 50 percent when the film was released. The hit film, therefore, brought about a fundamental change in the rodents' image.

Paradise for Horses

During a visit to Disneyland, most visitors will come across a passing horse-drawn carriage sooner or later. If you feel sorry for the animals, you can rest assured: Horse care is a top priority at Disney. The animals only work four hours a day, a maximum of four times a week. In addition, each of them has a beauty care program and an individual water trough. They wear a type of rubber shoe to ensure that the horses' hooves are also protected. Due to this, they won't hurt themselves on the stone floor, and in addition, the shoe provides a pleasant clattering sound when they walk past visitors.

Repeat Offender

In almost every single Pixar film, the voice of John Ratzenberger can be heard. His voice acting career at Pixar began as Hamm in *Toy Story* and then stretched to P.T. Flea from *A Bug's Life*, Mack from *Cars*, Tom from *Wall-E,* and Yeti from *Monsters University* – to name just a few of his roles. He seems to be so popular at Pixar that they included him in the film *Soul* with a cameo appearance – this time without a voice – as an Easter Egg.

Merida was the first Disney princess whose story wasn't actually based on an already existing one. Before, the stories of all Disney princesses had been inspired by various fairy tales or legends.

Disney in Italian

Usually, movie titles are also translated when a movie is to be released in another country. Most character names, on the other hand, are not changed at all or are only slightly adapted to make pronunciation easier. In Italy it was a bit different during the era of Benito Mussolini. At that time, the politician tried to make the Italian language free of foreign words. For this reason, famous Disney characters such as Mickey Mouse, Goofy, and Donald Duck were also given new names. Donald became Paperino, Goofy was named Pippo, and Mickey was known as Topolino.

Late Revenge

Before Mickey Mouse, Disney was represented by a mascot named Oswald the Lucky Rabbit. However, the rights to the bunny drawn by Walt Disney later went to a Universal Pictures producer named Charles Mintz (see page 22). Although the mouse, which took the bunny's place only a little later, is far more popular, the dislike for Mintz apparently persisted within the Disney corporation. The film *Up* makes this clear once again. The film's villain is based on the mascot thief by name. Charles Mintz became Charles Muntz for the film.

Family Dispute

In the final fight between Simba and Scar in *The Lion King,* one could almost assume that Simba is going to be defeated by his uncle. The idea is not entirely absurd, especially considering that it was initially planned that way. Scar was supposed to throw Simba off the king's rock. Simba should not really die, but for a brief moment it should look like Scar would win the fight. In addition, Scar was supposed to burst into hysterical laughter after his nephew had fallen and then he was to be engulfed by the surrounding flames. Thus, the scene could have looked even more dramatic than it does in the final version.

A Silent Love

The love story between Carl and Ellie, which is actually only briefly told in the film *Up*, is one of the most popular stories in a Pixar film. But if you pay close attention, you'll notice that Carl never says a word to his wife. In an early scene, Ellie is seen talking to him, but he says nothing back. Furthermore, the fast-forward of their time together is only accompanied by music but not by Carl's voice.

High Demands

It wasn't easy to satisfy Disney founder Walt Disney during his lifetime. At least when it came to working on the films, the company's animators had to repeatedly push themselves to their limits. Regarding *Pinocchio*, for example, the company boss demanded that the clocks in Geppetto's workshop were all to be created. Presenting design templates wasn't enough, as Walt Disney wanted to ensure the designs were logical and would actually work. Only when everything was perfect did he approve the designs.

Well-Deserved Break

While visitors to Disneyland in California spend their time on roller coasters and other attractions, park employees have to work. But at the park, they also have some opportunities to escape from their daily work routine and enjoy the pleasures of life. For example, they can head to the Matterhorn roller coaster to relax. They won't be allowed to ride the roller coaster, but the attraction holds a secret. There is a basketball hoop inside. Not visible to the park's guests, the employees can let off steam here.

A Sophisticated Technique

One detail on posters or other promotional items that feature several Disney princesses is very striking: They never seem to look at each other. There is a very special strategy behind this. The House of Mouse's marketing experts want to ensure that the princesses' respective worlds do not merge. Each princess should still stand for her own individual world. One major exception is the film *Ralph Breaks the Internet* – the sequel to *Wreck-It Ralph* – in which many Disney princesses meet in one scene.

An Alternate Stitch

A dangerous alien that gets stranded on a small island and undergoes significant personal development through a little girl – that's the story of *Lilo & Stitch*. However, only a few know that Stitch was originally planned quite differently. The character was actually created as early as 1985 as part of a planned children's book. Stitch was not supposed to be the result of an experiment but an intergalactic wanted criminal who got stranded in Kansas instead of Hawaii. In this version, Jumba did not appear as Stitch's creator but as a former member of his gang of criminals who was set on finding him.

Guest Appearances

Time and time again, fans burst into bright joy when they spot familiar Disney characters in other films. The little Easter Eggs appear in numerous movies and certainly influenced the fan theory that Disney films are all set in the same universe. A close look is rewarded: For example, the crowd celebrating the arrival of King Triton in an early scene of *The Little Mermaid* includes the familiar faces of Mickey, Goofy, and Donald.

Apparently, this is not the only big occasion to which foreign characters are invited: Rapunzel and Flynn Rider from *Tangled* also end up visiting the kingdom of Arendelle in *Frozen* when the royal house finally opens its doors.

In *Lilo & Stitch*, a poster of *Mulan* can be discovered on the wall of the room; Hercules boasts Scar's head from *The Lion King*; the Beast from *Beauty and the Beast* is shown as a character in *Aladdin*; Belle, Pumbaa, and Aladdin's flying carpet can be seen on the streets of Paris in *The Hunchback of Notre Dame*; and many more guest appearances are hidden in the different movies. If you feel like it, you can have fun tracking down all the hidden clues.

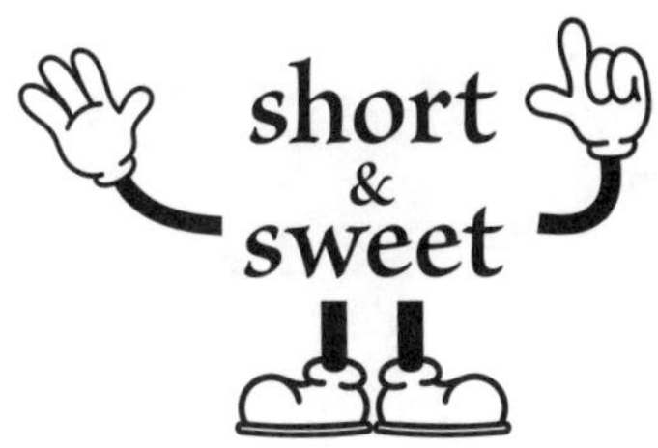

Merida is unique in many ways. One of the notable features that distinguishes her from the other Disney princesses is that she is a princess who doesn't sing once in her movie.

Alice in Wonderland was the first Disney animated film to make it to US television as a TV broadcast. The film was first shown to the general public in 1954.

Belle often has a strand of hair falling into her face, which apparently just won't stay where it should. The filmmakers used this peculiarity in Belle's design to show that even Disney princesses are not always perfect.

When Walt Disney died, he left his last words in writing. However, the last message from the company founder was very mysterious: "Kurt Russell." Neither the famous actor with this name nor anyone else knew what the Disney creator wanted to say with it.

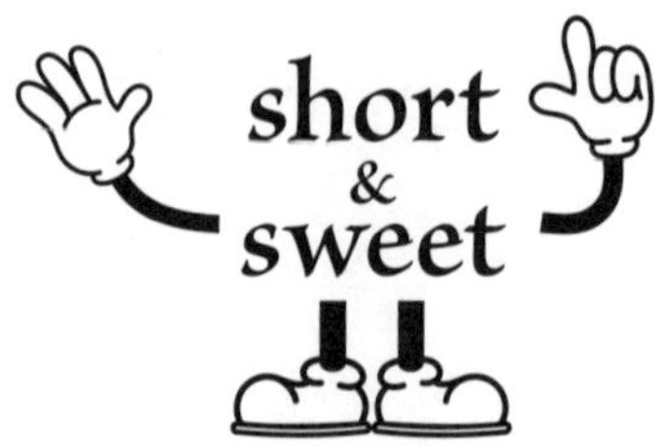

Rock legend Tina Turner took extra time off from her hiatus to sing the opening song of *Brother Bear.*

In order to shorten the plot of a film or make it a bit more straightforward, it sometimes happens that complete characters are removed from the story. This was also the case with *Aladdin*. Originally, Aladdin's mother was supposed to get a small role in the film, and Aladdin was even supposed to sing a song about her.

Disneyland sells an average of about two million turkey legs per year. Considering that a single thigh now costs around twelve dollars, this figure is nothing to sneeze at.

A flag from the twin towers of the World Trade Center can also be found at a Disney Park. It is located in the American Adventure Pavilion at Epcot.

Creepy Props

Not only the creators of Disney movies like to pay attention to details. A watchful eye is also directed to the little things in the theme parks of the House of Mouse. For example, some curiosities can be discovered when visiting some of the attractions. The Pirates of the Caribbean ride even featured real skeletons at some point. No, not just real-looking ones made of plastic. In the 1960s, when the attraction was created, the artificial pieces just didn't seem authentic enough to the people in charge, so they turned to the medical department of the University of California. There they purchased real human skeletons and placed them in the attraction as decoration. Nowadays, most of them have been removed and replaced by animatronic plastic skeletons.

Correct Display

Amateur historians get their money's worth when watching *Moana*. Several experts were consulted for the film, who recreated the starry sky over the Pacific Islands about 2,000 years ago. The characters' clothing was also meant to be historically accurate. That's why the outfits were all chosen as they would have looked 2,000 years ago. Even the materials available at the time were taken into account.

Remy as a Sommelier?

In the animated hit *Ratatouille,* it is revealed to film fans that (fictional) rats can even cook. Under certain circumstances, fans could have bought wine from this talented rat shortly afterward – or rather from the advertising experts behind it. After the film's success, a *Ratatouille*-themed wine was supposed to appear on the shelves of a supermarket chain. In the end, the project was scrapped because the film – unlike the wine – is aimed at a young audience. Those responsible feared that minors could also be motivated to drink the wine by referencing the animated hit.

A Film with Many Names

In most countries, the film about a young aspiring voyager is known as *Moana*. In some other regions, however, it bears the title *Vaiana*. Why it was released under different names is easily explained. *Moana* is not possible as a title in some countries because the name is associated with other things. In Italy, for example, a performer for films with adult content bears this name, and in the Netherlands, it is a registered brand name. Sometimes it's not so easy to name films the same way internationally.

A Canceled Appearance

Sometimes a certain idea is planned for a film, but in the end is never realized. For example, Nintendo mascot and star plumber Mario was originally supposed to appear in *Wreck-It Ralph*. In the end, however, the guest appearance did not happen because the makers remained undecided about incorporating the video game character into the film.

Blue Is Not Always the Same

A new project usually brings innovations in various fields. It may be a new way of working, an idea that will be used more often in the future, or a new color. A new color? Yes, even Disney's color lab always has innovations to show. For *The Little Mermaid*, a completely new shade of green and blue was created, which was later used for Ariel's fin. Of course, a new color needs an appropriate name. In keeping with its use, the shade was named Ariel.

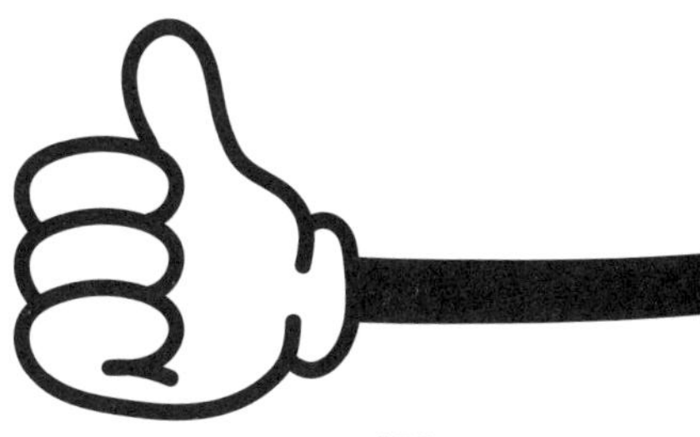

One Last Time

During his lifetime, Walt Disney was involved in the production of many films. The last Disney film that the company founder released himself was *The Aristocats*. The film is also the last to say "A Walt Disney Production" in the credits. For the following movie, *The Jungle Book*, Walt Disney could still be partially consulted, and some of his ideas for the film were implemented, but the founder died in 1966 before the film was finished.

The First Appearance

Mickey Mouse is not only one of the most famous Disney characters but also the mascot of the media giant. Since 2007, Mickey has appeared in a brief intro to Disney's animated films. Mickey can be seen whistling on a boat. However, this is not the first video of Mickey. His first appearance was in the short film *Plane Crazy*. The short, silent clip shows the little mouse trying to steer an airplane while being repeatedly interrupted by all sorts of difficulties. The nowadays better-known short film of Mickey on a steamship came only afterward.

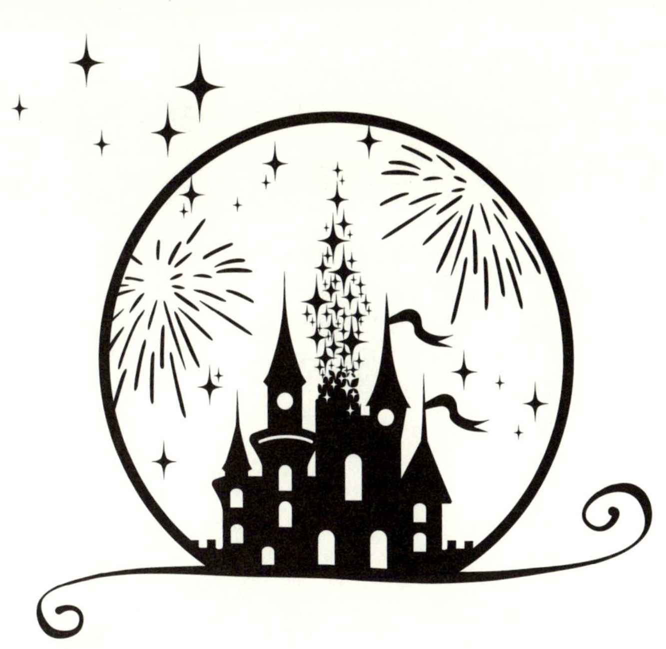

Different times, different rules. That was also the case with the premiere of *Snow White and the Seven Dwarfs* in the UK cinemas. The movie was rated "too scary," and children needed to be at least 16 years old to see the film. The only chance for younger fans to see the movie was to be accompanied by their parents.

Discover the Secrets of the Potter Universe!

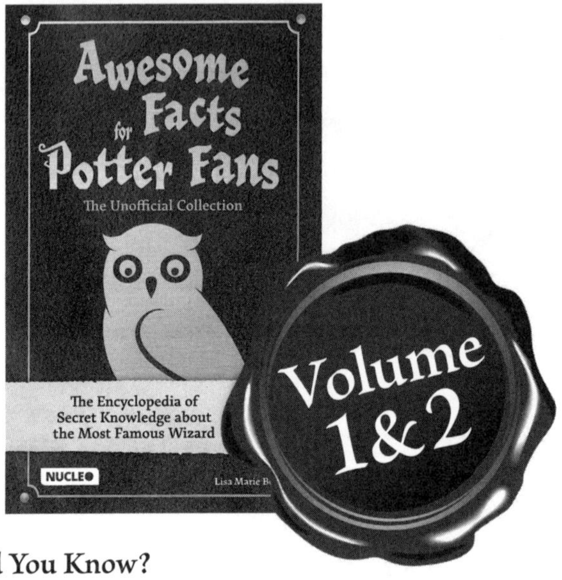

Did You Know?

A main character was supposed to die early.

One of the professors could have been a Quidditch pro.

The letter from Hogwarts doesn't even arrive on the 11th birthday.

Secret knowledge about the most famous wizard in the world awaits you.

Nearly 400 outstanding facts about the wizarding world make this book a must-have for every Potterhead. It will make you laugh, shake your head in disbelief, or simply leave you stunned and amazed.

Volume 1 & 2 of *Awesome Facts for Potter Fans* is available in stores.